# WATERWOGS
## and the Contested History of the
# GOLLIWOG

*Mr Golliwogg, with his Dutch doll friends, looking from behind a door in their first adventure.*

# WATERWOGS
## and the Contested History of the
# GOLLIWOG

*Todd Gray*

THE MINT PRESS

For Ken and Tamara,
who have never heard of the golliwogg



First published 2025

A publication of The Mint Press
Taddyforde House South
Taddyforde Estate
New North Road, Exeter EX4 4AT

www.stevensbooks.co.uk
01392 459760
sales@themintpress.co.uk

ISBN 978 1903 356 83 8

A CIP catalogue record for this book is available from the British Library



This publication is printed on acid-free paper

Typeset, printed and bound by Short Run Press Ltd, Exeter, Devon

# Contents


| | | |
|---|---|---|
| Preface | | 7 |
| Acknowledgments | | 9 |
| INTRODUCTION | | 11 |
| CHAPTER 1: | The Waterwog | 17 |
| CHAPTER 2: | Origins: Florence Upton's golliwogg, 1895-1909 | 23 |
| | Inspiration | 30 |
| | Features | 37 |
| | Financial imperative | 42 |
| | Ugliness | 44 |
| CHAPTER 3: | Appropriation | 51 |
| | Enid Blyton, 1926-1986 | 51 |
| | Other appropriators | 55 |
| CHAPTER 4: | The Robertson's golly, 1915-2002 | 69 |
| | Under pressure | 77 |
| CHAPTER 5: | Race | 83 |
| | Two concurrent perspectives | 99 |
| CHAPTER 6: | Golliwogs abroad | 109 |
| | The United States | 109 |
| | The British Empire | 116 |
| | Australasia | 118 |
| CHAPTER 7: | Infatuation, the 1900s and 1910s | 125 |
| CHAPTER 8: | Permeating society, the 1920s to the 1940s | 139 |
| CHAPTER 9: | Falling out of favour, the 1950s and 1960s | 149 |
| | The 1950s | 149 |
| | The 1960s | 153 |

| | |
|---|---|
| CHAPTER 10: The golliwog's demise, 1970 to 2001 | 159 |
| The 1970s and 1980s | 160 |
| Unease | 162 |
| The 1990s and the new millennium | 166 |
| CONCLUSION | 171 |
| Illustration sources | 185 |
| References | 189 |
| Index | 209 |

# Preface

I saw my first golliwog on the morning of 14 July 1973 in a kitchen in Ilford. I was on a school trip from the United States and was being introduced to marmalade when I spotted the little figure on the jar. I was astonished, transfixed and mortified. My hosts were perplexed. Five years later I returned to England and was equally surprised by *The Black and White Minstrel Show*. It was another example of how English sensibilities differed from those back in New England. Over the following years friends occasionally blacked-up for parties and, once again, no thought was given to racial denigration. Since then Britain has become ethnicity-aware but I retain vivid memories of how crucial individual circumstances are in shaping our perceptions of race.

I have subsequently learned, as a historian, that personal experiences and senses of identity are often the most important factors in forming the history we are able to accept. I appreciate that the historical evidence both supports and challenges the two main views of golliwogs in our polarised society, but I hope there is still a consensus that a considered investigation of the wider historical evidence is the most effective means of accessing the past.

*Taddyforde, 1 January 2025*

*Face, for a soft toy, made from moulded and stiffened black felt with two glass eyes, c1953.*

# Acknowledgments

I would like to thank Anti Racist Cumbria, Archives & Special Collections (University of Glasgow), Bernie Grant Trust, Bishopsgate Institute, the Robert L. Bogomolny Library (University of Baltimore), Badge Collectors' Circle, British Balloon Museum & Library, British Film Institute, Bromley Local History Society, Civilian Aviation Authority, Green Left, Jim Crow Museum, Liverpool City Council, Merrythought, National Council of Negro Women, Paisley Museum, Searchlight Archive (University of Northampton), Special Collections Research Center (Charles Library, Temple University), Spielzeugmuseum (Nuremburg), Tameside Local Studies and Archive Centre, Time Out Media, Virtual War Memorial Australia and the Young V&A for assistance with this project. Freedom of Information requests were made to the Equality & Human Rights Commission, Royal Borough of Greenwich, Islington Council and Liverpool City Council. Images, which appear mostly through the permission of private collectors and other owners or acknowledged copyright holders, are noted separately.

Amongst those individuals who have particularly helped are Elly Babbedge, Professor Eddie Chambers, Matthew Crampton, Alan Massey, Joe Mills, Charlotte Nightingale and Frank Setchfield as well as Beryl Bletcher, Jill Drysdale, Ann Franklin, Carole Herbert, Judith Hosking, Sue Jackson and Dr John Sealey who have shared their memories. Some others prefer to remain anonymous. I am grateful to Professor Jonathan Barry, Dr Ryan Hanley, Sue Jackson, Dr Andrew Thrush and Dr Ruth Vasey who have read parts or the entirety of this text and who have made many helpful comments. All remaining errors are, of course, of my own making. Finally, I would like to thank Keith Stevens for his continuing support.

**Note**

Some historic language is challenging. Words, which form parts of quotations and were once normalised language but are now widely viewed as being offensive, appear in amended forms, e.g., n*gger and w*g. The longer spelling of 'golliwogg' is reserved for Upton's original character whereas the shorter 'golliwog' refers to his subsequent incarnation. 'Golly' is used in reference to Robertson's figure.

# INTRODUCTION

Many people shudder upon hearing the word 'golliwog', but it makes others feel wistful and nostalgic. This division lies at the heart of how this figure is viewed in modern Britain. How did it become so divisive and can an understanding of its history not only help bridge these two polarised views but act as a prism through which we can understand the development of race relations in Britain? Those questions are the essence of this book.

Uncertainty greeted the first appearance of the golliwogg in 1895 but children were drawn to him and then, most surprisingly to adults, he was widely adored. Six decades later the golliwog was reappraised and condemned amongst growing feelings of resentment and scorn. Today he is a passing memory rather than a living part of society and his features have not retained the racialised resonance they once had. His reputation, however, remains chequered. Surprisingly, the multifaceted nature of his broader history, from golliwogg to golliwog to golly, is unknown even as the figure remains fiercely contested.

The golliwogg is a British invention, but one born with American ancestry. Four generations ago it comprehensively embedded itself into popular culture: golliwogs have been referenced by James Joyce in *Ulysses,* Kurt Vonnegut in *Slaughterhouse-Five,* Ian Fleming in *Chitty Chitty Bang Bang* and by H. G. Wells, G. K. Chesterton, Aldous Huxley, E. M. Forster, E. F. Benson and Elinor Glyn amongst many other authors. They inspired music including, most notably, a suite for piano by Claude Debussy; as a child Jackie Kennedy danced her first ballet to his 'Golliwog Cakewalk' and she was, curiously, called 'that golliwog of a child' by Franklin Roosevelt's daughter. A wide range of commercial products featuring golliwogs were manufactured in this country and overseas.[1] In 1956 the *Wide World Magazine* reported unexpected consequences:

> 'One would hardly think a label on a tin could cause trouble. Yet, an African came into a District Commissioner's office saying that he could prove without doubt that the White man ate African children, and not only that, but canned the meat and sold it! He held up a tin of meat on the label of which there was a picture of a golliwog! Eventually the label was changed by the manufacturers but not before a great many natives had seen it or had heard of it or passed the story on to their friends'.[2]

Pets, racing horses and yachts were named Golliwog as well as a daffodil, varieties of gloxinia (*Sinningia aggregate*) and daylily (*Hemerocallis*) and *Callisia Repens* is also known as the Golliwog Plant.[3]

It is impossible to imagine the range of unusual scenarios which have involved golliwogs. For instance, in 1914 a desperate British air pilot, who had run short of bombs, dropped his golliwog onto a German battleship, in 1939 a dozen New Zealand golliwogs were sent to a leper colony in the Fiji Islands, in 1944, after a German doodlebug exploded in London, rescuers searched rubble strewn with golliwogs, in 1945 General Eisenhower was given a red, white and blue golliwog with American army buttons on his waistcoat, in 1951 'Johnny the Golliwog', a ventriloquist's dummy, taught bible lessons in St Albans because 'it is possible in this way to explain to children passages which the teachers normally find difficult to make them understand' and in 1952 an Australian cow was named Golliwog.[4]

Amongst these unexpected connections lies a Bedfordshire couple's belief in 1973 that they owed fifty years of married bliss to a golliwog. In 1922 Sam Clark had picked up a rag doll which a toddler threw out of a pushchair and returned it to her sister whom he married a year later.[5] In 1979 the favourite dance partner of Sylvia Hampson (1919-2016) was a six-foot golliwog she had made from foam rubber and old curtains. The married housewife from Brecon explained: 'Beneath his feet are elastic hoops and when I want to dance, I put my feet into the loops and the golliwog comes with me'. Her husband Jeffrey did not mind them dancing at home or his wife taking the golliwog to public dances: 'I'm not jealous of a golliwog, even one this size. It relieves me of having to dance these days'. She added 'I love dancing and now I can simply put on a record and dance to my heart's content. And Golly is a much better dancer than my husband. He never steps on my toes'.[6]

Many associations raise questions which will likely stay unanswered. For instance, it would be interesting to know more of the motivation behind a Welsh boarding house-keeper's decision to decorate her home with golliwogs; Mrs Kate Reason (1854-1933) papered the entirety of her guests' lavatory at Pleasant View in Llanfairfechan with hundreds of golly labels from Robertson's marmalade. Had she a surplus of marmalade jars which had been emptied by her visitors in the 1920s?[7] Equally, what were the thoughts of those Black women in Birmingham who, during the 1950s and 1960s, earned a living from enamelling golly badges?[8]

Amongst these curious happenings, on an everyday basis golliwogs were found in children's bedrooms, placed on breakfast tables and featured in adverts. The golliwog's significance lay in how it permeated Britain across its classes, age groups and regions. It was omnipresent for more than a century. The golliwog's continuing popularity in 1954 prompted one observer to comment 'he is among the immortals'. Yet today's surviving golliwogs are largely secreted away out-of-sight and are all but forgotten in a wave of collective amnesia.

Its modern scarcity is the consequence of the golliwog having become divisive for more than half of its one-hundred-and-thirty-year history. It neatly exemplifies just how differently a cultural aspect can be viewed. Unwelcome to some will be the news that Devon developed its own version but it is possible that a fresh examination of the historical evidence, prompted by this discovery of a previously overlooked element, might help reconcile polarised opinions.

As the golliwog embedded itself in society, it became the most visible representation of a Black man or woman. Our understanding of it can be broadened by considering its long history, particularly the varied permutations that it took, and also its origins, role, place and popularity as a named fairy-tale character, rag doll, trademark and caricature.

The memory of this figure is passing. An airing of the two divergent perspectives of today's senior generation, which was directly impacted by the golliwog, reveals this figure's part in the growth of race awareness. This will be examined in relation to the creation of the golliwog when Britain was at the epicentre of the largest empire the world has ever seen and the instilling in the overwhelmingly White population a sense of racial dominion and proprietorship. Also discussed is the golliwog's demise following the immigration which transformed Britain into a multi-cultural country in terms of race and religion.

Society has, since then, reevaluated and redefined its wider history but this is the first broad historical examination of the golliwog. This figure has been the focus of more than one hundred thousand news reports, appeared in several hundred children's books, stories and poems as well as in dozens of stage plays, dances and songs. It has been discussed in more than four hundred academic articles and social commentary pieces and has been the subject of a doctoral thesis. Despite this coverage, interest has been largely contained to journalists, social commentators, sociologists and literature specialists and the broader history of the golliwog has, until now, remained ignored by historians.[9]

*1a. The Golliwogg, 1901.*

# CHAPTER 1

# The Waterwog

Until recently Exeter had forgotten its waterwog, the city's own version of the golliwog.

The golliwog's recent passing has obscured its longer history: he embarrasses the British public which prefers to forget the place he established in society. This includes the notable enthusiasm during the First World War when he was taken up as a lucky mascot by servicemen. In 1914 a soldier waved his 'ferocious-looking' golliwog at a crowd which had gathered to watch a column of Canadians march down the High Street in Exeter. Hundreds of thousands of golliwogs were then being made by hand across the country, sold for charity and sent as good luck charms to loved ones at the front. Teddy bears, horseshoes, four-leaf-clovers, rabbits' feet, touchwoods and black cats were also considered lucky but golliwogs were the most popular. In 1916 the readers of a Toronto newspaper had a progress report on one such mascot from 'somewhere in Belgium':

> 'You ask about Claude. He is getting on very well. The boys are contemplating washing his white waistcoat as it was covered with oil in a recent bombardment. He is as famous out here as he seems to be at home, having been spoken to lately by one of the British generals'.[10]

It was during the first months of the war that the Exeter War Relief Committee created 'waterwogs'. They were referred to as the golliwog's 'blood relations'. In 1914 twenty-five out-of-work

*1b. Servicemen in the trenches opening a mail package, 1917. The caption noted 'these great warriors rock with laughter at the surprise of a comrade to whom someone in Blighty has sent a golliwog'.*

young women from the collar factory were employed at Palace Gate to manufacture these figures from Egyptian loofah. They were intended to be used by children during bathtime:

> 'To drop a golliwog in the water was to spoil him, but the waterwog delights in it and the fact that he is as equable and good-natured in the water as on dry land should serve to make the tub more attractive to his little master or mistress'.

One commentator asked 'the name, in all conscience, is unwieldy, bizarre enough, but, after all, what's in a name?' He noted their inspiration:

> 'One does not have to carry the mind very far back to remember a black-faced, keen-eyed little fellow for whom the younger generation were wont to display a great affection and whom even those who had passed the stage of adolescence did not affect to despise.'

The waterwog's appearance was:

> 'Scarcely so perky in appearance, hardly so winning as his predecessor, students of anatomy may cavil at the want of symmetry in his proportions and lovers of the aesthetic may not pronounce the disposition of his features a thing of beauty and a joy for ever. But for all that, he is an appealing little person and will doubtless find his way straight to the juvenile heart.'

The waterwog did not look like the traditional golliwog but neither did the Great War golliwog charms. The waterwog, also called the 'loofah doll', was invented by Kate Noddall (1862-1932) and possibly her sister Frances of 10 Higher Summerlands. There was also a loofah duck, possibly a rival, which had been designed by another woman.

The cessation of German imports of toys created an opportunity for British entrepreneurs across the country to utilise the unemployed, including women, and invalided and wounded servicemen in toy-making. Thus, the Exeter scheme was similar to another based in Gorleston-on-Sea in Norfolk. Two unmarried women turned to toy-making to relieve unemployment in the seaside resort. Amongst the toys they made were golliwogs and other 'freak animals' designed by one of the women.[11] Other young women were employed making dolls across England, including in Devon at Great Torrington, and specifically golliwogs in places such as Newport in Shropshire and Ramsgate in Kent.

The adaption of the word golliwog was also not unique to Exeter. In 1914 the 'walliwog' was created by Rev. Francis Jewell (1838-1925) of Prestatyn in Wales. He perceived golliwogs as being artificial and 'wretched little things that ladies wore on their shoulders and took great delight in kissing upon the least provocation as a sort of practice for something better in the future'. His walliwogs were made naturally from remnants of trees and their roots 'in many curious forms and fantastic shapes' which bore a resemblance to living creatures. The effect upon the observer, he suggested, was the thought 'What comical little creatures they are'. They were, he explained, the antecedents of golliwogs. Jewell was called an ardent lover of nature by his obituarist.[12]

It is not known how successful waterwogs were or whether their manufacture continued after the war but there was sufficient confidence in them for the figure to be patented. It is likely that production ceased in 1918 or 1919. The waterwog passed from memory even as its predecessor advanced in popularity. It is not uncommon today to meet former Exeter children who had happily played with their golliwogs but after more than a century no memories survive from any child who once owned a waterwog.[13] Several generations after the waterwog's creation, children's sponges in the shape of golliwogs were again for sale in Exeter; in 1979 and 1980 they were sold by Boots the Chemist.[14]

How does this curious phase in the history of the golliwog, the waterwog, fit into modern perceptions? Many, if not most, modern children and teenagers are personally unfamiliar with the golliwog, if not baffled by it, but the remainder of society is divided. One portion remembers their childhood toys with fondness and, crucially, many recount that they were unaware of a racial association. Another segment condemns golliwogs as a denigrating emblem, the most potent British symbol of racism. They also link them with the shortened version of the word which a century ago became derogatory. These divergent perspectives make the golliwog's history contested.

Race awareness has changed markedly over the last four generations. By 1914, when the waterwog made its appearance, *Little Black Sambo* had been popular for more than a dozen years.

The waterwog was created more than a century ago but it seems unbelievable now that within living memory shoes, polish, wool, fabric and even cars were sold as 'n*gger brown' and that until 1978 the prime spot on BBC television was given to *The Black and White Minstrel Show.* For twenty years this company of White performers used blackface, the theatrical makeup used to 'black up', in order to portray southern American Black men in what was an award-winning light entertainment programme broadcast on Saturday evenings. It began broadcasting in 1958 by which time the golliwog was being questioned, the British Empire was disintegrating and Caribbean immigration was fundamentally altering Britain's ethnic character. It was during these years that long-standing elements of the nation's culture, including the golliwog, were reappraised. For many, this matter has been uneasily addressed but not satisfactorily resolved.[15] To this mix we can now add the waterwog.

The waterwog is a reminder that significant elements of our history can be easily overlooked and that these aberrant strands can help society understand how it has been shaped and moulded. It raises many questions including those around how it fits into modern Britain's perception of the golliwog.

*2a. The Golliwogg, Florence Upton's creation.*

## CHAPTER 2

# Origins: Florence Upton's golliwogg, 1895-1909

The genesis of the golliwogg came in the last years of the reign of Victoria when the British Empire was still expanding.

Imaginative, if not far-fetched, explanations have been given for the origins of the word golliwogg including that it was a mispronunciation of dolly, that it combined dolly with wag, that it originated as a name for singers in Kentucky and that 'it is said to have been also used of a band of men in the Southern States of America somewhat resembling the Ku Klux Klan'. Others have wrongly claimed that it was derived from the Indian words *golly*, meaning a tall person, and w*g, 'a black fellow'.[16] Perhaps not surprisingly, it has sometimes been attributed to pollywog, the American alternative word for a tadpole 'which the doll with its large black head resembles'. The most imaginative explanation was given in 1996 by the owner of an American doll shop. She decided the original golliwog was 'an entertainer in England who dressed as a clown and was immortalised by a Toulouse-Lautrec painting'.[17]

However, without question the golliwogg, as a word and character, was invented in Britain in 1895. An Edwardian commentator recognised this was 'a genuine creation' of Miss Florence Kate Upton (1873-1922) who had conceived the figure when she decided to write a children's book and exclaimed 'He

*2b. Above: The first appearance of The Golliwogg; he introduces himself to two of the Dutch dolls, 1895.*

*3. Left: Florence Upton, aged 23 in 1896.*

*4. Below: The ambulance which was purchased through the sale of Upton's rag doll, 1917.*

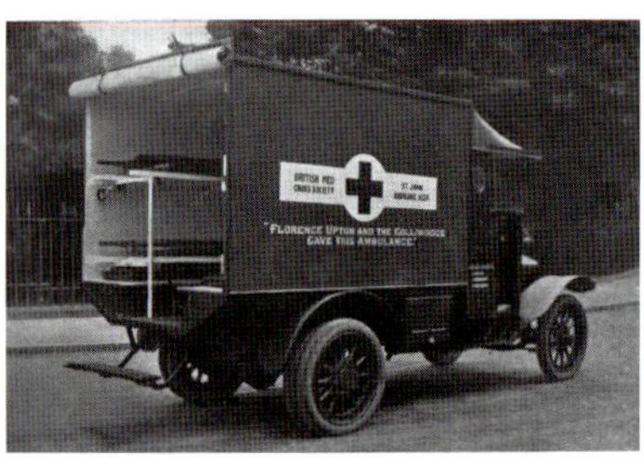

will be my hero. I will call him Golliwogg'. Upton recalled of the name:

> 'The actual origin is difficult to explain; it came of itself. As the Golliwogg has always seemed to me to be telling me his own biography, so in the same way he must have told me his own name, for one day, when the pictures were about half completed, and the verses not yet begun, I picked him up from the table in my studio, and without intention of naming him, without the idea of a name passing through my mind, I called him *Golliwogg*'.

She added 'he seemed Golliwogg, he *was* Golliwogg. Ask yourself, *could* he have had any other name?' Upton explained 'I remember, I did not think the name pretty, any more than I had thought the face beautiful, and I even hesitated when it came to throwing him upon the world with such a name.'[18]

Upton had recently moved from America to England and may not have been consciously aware of her word's associations and origins. She may have had unwitting knowledge that 'golly', an alternative word for God, was commonly used to indicate comic surprise in black caricatures. It was regarded in the United States as being Black dialect: an etymological dictionary defined it as a 'Negro perversion of God'. Was this a subliminal connection in the recesses of Upton's thoughts when she named the Golliwogg? Moreover, did she blend it with pollywog in intentional or unfortunate cultural appropriation?[19]

By 1908 golliwog had become part of common language when an Australian commented 'The word has eaten its way into our speech as the thing had penetrated to the heart of our national life, that it came by way of the nursery cannot alter the fact.' But he was mystified by its origins:

> 'Golliwogs are nothing if not modern. They are the product of a complex and slightly morbid mind, we should say; certainly

a mind of our own time. Possibly they were so named on the principle which guided Eve in naming the toad at the beginning of things. The toad was called a toad because it looked like a toad.'

Upton's word evolved: almost immediately upon its appearance golly became a common concurrent shortening of golliwogg and this was later picked up by Robertson's, the preserves and marmalade firm.[20] The word was played with by writers including in 1909 when short stories featured a 'boyliwog', a 'girliwog' and a 'nursiwog'.[21]

In 1895 Upton was twenty-two-years-old and, although born in New York to English parents, was living in London when the golliwogg burst into life in *The Adventures of Two Dutch Dolls and a 'Golliwogg'*. She illustrated the book and her mother Bertha (1849-1912) wrote the verses. The golliwogg became their most popular character; one reviewer wrote that summer:

'The words are clever and funny but it is the illustrations that are the strong point of the work. These are more than clever, for with a wonderfully skilful touch the artist has contrived to give an extraordinarily truthful human expression to the faces, figures and attitudes of just such hard, unreal wooden dolls as may be bought in any cheap toy-shop for a penny a piece. And with these conventional puppets Miss Florence Upton has associated the grotesque, ludicrous Golliwogg, with his black face and fuzzy hair – a figure that seems to have just stepped out of a Jack-in-the-Box.'[22]

Another reviewer concluded of this first book:

'An attempt at description would be little short of ridiculous; every page of verse and action reveals something new and strange in the line of the possibilities of the genius of absurdity.'[23]

In 1901 a subsequent book, *The Golliwogg's Air-Ship,* received high praise in the *Times of India*:

> 'Last year the wonderful adventures of that strange being, the Golliwogg, were followed with bated breath by thousands of children who will be eager to again see the large-headed black-haired gentleman. The Golliwogg reappears absolutely up to date, *for he has visited an aeronaut who told me all he knew*... The Golliwogg is, indeed, a wonderful being and it is to be hoped that he will continue his adventurous career for many years.'[24]

Upton's publisher described her hero as 'the great black golliwogg' but most reviewers refrained from commenting upon race. Those that did include a writer in *The Churchman* who thought in 1902 that the golliwogg was 'a Negro monstrosity with Eskimo hair'. Another in 1896 regarded him as the hero who 'represents, we imagine, the unbreakable, rag species of our youth and he is, moreover, black, with a ferocious black wig'.[25] Four years later a reviewer of the dolls' Polar adventures wrote 'the black face of the golliwogg in white fur is simply delightful'. In 1905 one writer listed his caricatured features but appeared unaware of them: 'that fearsome-looking doll with the big red mouth, the staring eyes and the tousled black hair'. Others referred to him as 'that young gentleman', 'inimitable', 'the fascinating monster', the dolls' 'monster friend', 'that queer creation', 'a weird, black-visaged doll of high renown', 'that black sprite', 'a hideous black rag doll', 'the whimsical Golliwogg and his curious family' and that there were 'few stranger and more delightful flowers of a young girl's imagination than Miss Upton's creation'.[26] A dozen years after Upton's first book one reviewer made an unusual observation: 'Age cannot stale nor custom wither the infinite variety of Monsieur Golliwogg and his attendant ladies. Fortunate man to have such devoted *houris*, albeit of the Dutch doll kind, to wait on his every pleasure'.[27] It was about this time that another writer thought 'though the hero is grotesque, his courage and goodwill counterbalance his lack of external beauty'.[28]

In Upton's story the golliwogg makes his first appearance when a box of dolls came to life on Christmas Eve. Suddenly:

'Then all look round, as well they may
To see a horrid sight!
The blackest gnome
Stands there alone,
They scatter in their fright.

With kindly smile he nearer draws;
Begs them to feel no fear.
*What is your name*?
Cries Sarah Jane;
*The Golliwogg, my dear*.

Their fears allayed - each takes an arm,
While up and down they walk;
With sidelong glance
Each tries her chance,
And charms him with small talk.'

A London reviewer commented in 1895:

'I must confess that I am a little curious to make the acquaintance of that Golliwog. What is it? Is it a Lewis Carrolian creature from behind the looking-glass, or an importation from Wonderland, or merely a polliwig, with a difference?'[29]

Shortly afterwards another critic observed that the Golliwogg, the hero with the 'wonted shirt-button eyes, no nose and portentous red mouth' who had a 'hirsute and ferocious aspect', had 'come to stay'. It was felt that he had become a naturalised citizen in the land of Christmas books.[30]

*5. Right: Two American minstrels in blackface, c1900.*

## Inspiration

Upton was born eight years after the end of American slavery but when the civil rights of Black men and women remained restricted. She based the golliwogg on her own childhood rag doll which an aunt had rediscovered in 1894 being stored in her London home. Twenty-three years later it was auctioned to raise funds for a Red Cross ambulance; it was marked 'Florence Upton and the Golliwoggs gave this ambulance'. The purchaser deposited the doll at Chequers which later became the prime ministers' country retreat. It is now in the collection of the Young V&A in London. That doll's leather face has a triangular nose, large white eyes and vivid red lips which are thinner than the later commercial golliwog dolls.

*6. Upton's original doll, a soft toy made of stuffed brown cloth with a face of black leather. This humanoid figure has white buttons for eyes, a triangular nose of leather and his mouth comprises two red stitched lines. His hair is made from animal fur. He wears red felt trousers, a white cotton shirt with a red bow and a long-sleeved blue jacket with tailcoats.*

There was imaginative speculation in 1917 on the origins of Upton's doll: she claimed it came from an American fair but it was speculated that the 'lovable fright, the golliwog, is the direct descendant of an old African idol carried to America in the dark days, but his genealogy is a little doubtful'.[31] Upton's golliwogg initially wore the doll's red trousers, white shirt, blue jacket and red bow tie.

Upton's doll had different British and American cultural associations. During the late eighteenth century,

"WHAT FOR YOU HANG DE PICKANINNY?"

*7. Engraving highlighting earlier racial sensitivities, 1839.*

and throughout the nineteenth, black dolls were most commonly associated in Britain with street signs for dealers in rags.[32] In the early 1800s some of these merchants deployed 'n*ggerly dialect' to advertise their shops: in one advert of 1846 a 'dark gentleman' asked '*Why Dinah, do all the people come to Massa's shop*?' upon which she replied '*Because Sambo Massa gives the best price…*'[33]

The dolls had literary depictions. In 1839 the *Comic Annual* included a critic's appraisal of a 'droll' story in which racial denigration is wrongly perceived:

> 'the indignation of a Negro, on passing an old rag-shop, the insignia of which, everyone knows, is a black doll. But Mungo, imagining that an insult was intended to all his sable fraternity,

waxed wrath at the sight of the obnoxious emblem, and giving vent to his outraged feelings through stentorian lungs, he brought the queen of rags to the shop door, to know who dared to find fault with the jetty symbol, which had till then swung at its ease wantoning in the breeze, when the ears of its mistress were saluted by Brother Blacky exclaiming *What for you hang de picaninny*? at the same time raising threateningly his cudgel high in the air.'[34]

Another story, 'The Black Doll', appeared in a journal in 1874[35] and *Jimmy Scenes from the Life of a Black Doll told by Himself* was published in 1888, seven years before Upton's first book. The main character is a Black boy sailor who recounts his life as a nursery toy.[36]

Black dolls were also exhibited outside marine-store shops and according to one late Victorian they:

'originated when formerly cast-off clothes were bought in large quantities for the purpose of being shipped to uncivilised countries and a black doll gaily dressed was exhibited in front of the shops of dealers in cast-off garments as a sign that the proprietor dealt in such goods for exportation to Africa.'[37]

Golliwogs had another British forebear in Aunt Sally, the early nineteenth-century fairground figure who held a clay tobacco pipe in her mouth as balls or cudgels were pelted at her. She was described in 1862 as 'a large, black, wooden doll of unlovely aspect with goggle eyes, gaping mouth'. That year a commentator asked two pertinent questions:

'Is there any secret antipathy of the White race towards the Black which is thus surreptitiously indulged? Or is there a deeper meaning still and does the black-visaged one represent Mumbo Jumbo and her assailants symbolise the victory of White virtue over Black vice?'[38]

8. *Two Black dandies, 1890.*

However, the inspiration for Upton's doll, and by extension the golliwogg, was not the British black doll or Aunt Sally. Neither was it, as one writer supposed, Peter, the Dutch black-faced assistant to St Nicholas. Instead, there has been widespread agreement that it depicted the American White minstrels who used blackface.[39] Both the golliowgg and the doll featured dark-coloured skin and shaggy hair, bright thickened lips and pop eyes. From the 1830s until the 1880s these performers entertained White audiences by presenting a version of enslaved Africans in Southern estates. These caricatures were not only given to thievery and cowardice but were indolent, shiftless, overtly-sexual, superstitious and lacking in intelligence. This view was captured by William Chambers (1800-1883), the Scottish publisher, who toured the United States just before the Civil War and summed up the characteristics of the Black race as having 'The want of mental energy and forethought, the love of finery and trifling amusements, distaste of persevering industry and bodily labour, as well as the overpowering animal propensities.'

The Upton family lived just outside New York City in Flushing and had easy access to theatres but it is not known if they were entertained by American minstrels who at that time were becoming less popular. It is possible that teenage-Upton was unaware of the minstrels or even misunderstood her doll's cultural connotations. She may have associated her doll with the Black Dandy, the finely-dressed and well-tailored figure who was ridiculed as being over-dressed by White commentators. While the minstrels have normally been associated with Upton's figure it may be useful to describe the inspiration as 'Minstrel Dandies'.

Thomas Dartmouth Rice (1808-1860) was the first American minstrel to visit Exeter in 1840, seventy-five years before the waterwog was created. Rice was known as the 'father of minstrelsy' because of his famous and most enduring blackface character, 'Jumping' Jim Crow. One reviewer noted Rice:

> 'has all the appearance of a real American n*gger and his representation of the character of that race is original and highly entertaining. He is very tall, has a powerful voice, with a humorous expression of countenance which cannot fail to promote the risible faculties: added to this he has a fund of dry humour'.

Twenty-seven years later, in 1867, Exeter saw first-hand those individuals whom Rice had parodied. The Great American Slave Troupe comprised sixteen formerly-enslaved men who played banjos and sang ditties 'in that peculiar and mirth-provoking manner characteristic of the Negro race'. Professional White and Black minstrel shows continued in Britain on stage until the early 1900s when competition came in the form of movies and music hall. In the United States vaudeville overwhelmed the minstrel tradition but British music hall often included minstrel performers as part of a wider programme. Minstrel shows, at the time of the appearance of the golliwogg in 1895, were becoming confined in Britain to amateur stages or at the seaside. This changed in 1958 when for the following twenty years they appeared on television and in 1962 the *Black and White Minstrel*

*9. Lantern slide photograph of two White men in blackface using the word 'Golly' in what was intended as a humorous manner, 1890.*

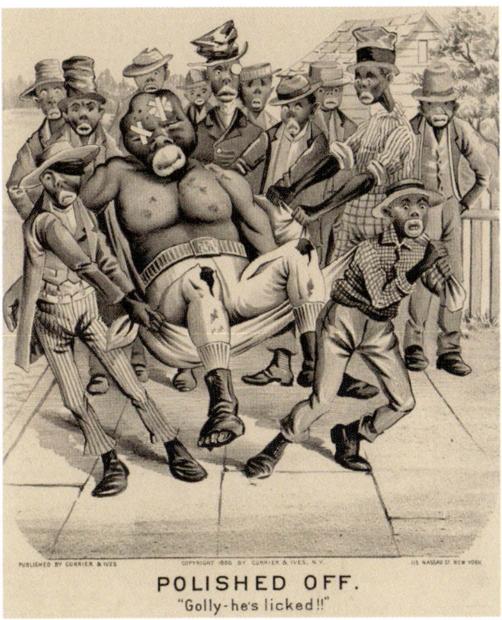


*10. A defeated boxer being carried by caricatured men with the comic use of the term 'Golly', 1888.*

*Show* ran at the Victoria Palace in London for seven years with nearly 5,000 performances.[40]

At the time of the publication of Upton's first book an entertainment took place twenty miles from Exeter in the village of Spreyton where local men and women performed in the schoolroom. This event demonstrates the popularity of the minstrel tradition before the appearance of the golliwogg. One journalist reported the:

> 'n*gger songs and business were enthusiastically received and repeatedly encored, particularly in the 'Alabama Coon' where two coal-black dolls (life size) took an inanimate part in the performance and the be-ribboned banjo added greatly to the effect of 'Old Folks at Home'.

This show also establishes a use of the black doll in minstrel performances. At this time they were in Exeter toy shops including Wreford & Son ('rag dolls, wax dolls, washing dolls, sleeping dolls, large dolls, small dolls, dressed dolls, white or black dolls and baby dolls'). Black dolls had been sold in Devon, as in the rest of the country, for many years previous to the creation of the golliwogg.[41]

**Features**

Upton featured the golliwogg in another twelve books over the course of fourteen years and his clothing depended upon his adventures.[42] Upton's golliwogg was a doll and a humanoid: he was a towering, ungainly and over-sized gnome without hands or feet. Mr Golliwogg, or sometimes The Golliwogg, was a dehumanised character who existed in the charmed world of make-believe with living dolls and toys such as jack-in the-boxes,

*11. Opposite page: Examples of Florence Upton's depictions of the Golliwogg's adventures, 1896-1909.*

scissor-boys and hobby horses. In 1913 one writer noted that the golliwogg was the form of a child's dreams, these 'beings that live just beyond the ken of the five senses are something more than a pleasing diversion, they are a help and solace in time of trouble'.[43]

Sambo was another of Upton characters; he was a banjo-playing singing minstrel doll in human form. His clothes were finer than those of the golliwogg and he was Black in contrast to Mr Golliwogg who had grey skin (probably to distinguish it from his mass of black hair which had varying shapes and length). Most commentators regarded black skin and unruly hair as the golliwog's two defining features. In 1896, a year after his first appearance, the Fancy Costume Ball in Glasgow included 'here and there the black face and enormous head of hair of the golliwogg'.

*13. Stanton, a golliwog in 1920.*

Hair was most often singled out for comment and comparison. In 1907 when a child in the London Underground saw an old man with 'thick, rather woolly-looking hair brushed up all round his forehead' he observed 'there's a white golliwogg'.[44]

*12. Opposite page: Harold Chapman in drag with Mark Leslie as a golliwog, for the Bow Belles, c1910-1919. In 1932 Leslie performed in character at a party given by the Duchess of Westminster.* The Tatler *reported on 10 February that Prince George, Duke of Kent, enjoyed the dancing more than any other guest.*

Having disorderly hair was also the supposed reason for the M. P. Charles Butt Stanton (1873-1946) being called a golliwog in parliament. Stanton was known for his 'tremendous shock of iron-grey hair'.[45] In 1960 an observer of the 'wild, wild' hair of Ken Dodd (1927-2018) quipped 'I'm told when he goes to the hairdresser's for his golliwog trim, he has to be smuggled out a side door. Otherwise the hairdresser might lose all his customers!'[46]

Men and women were nicknamed golliwog and also casually referred to as a golliwog. A dictionary printed in 1948 defined a golliwog as 'a grotesque person reminding one of the golliwog dolls'.[47] In many instances the association was made when lightly mocking White men and women who flouted social convention by having wild hair. Fashionable women's hairstyles that were unusually high or frizzy gave rise to comparisons with golliwogs throughout the twentieth century. In 1931 the coiffure which won the Grand Prix at the International Hairdressing competition in Paris was won by an English hairdresser for her permanent wave. The London model had reservations: 'I return to the cubicle and see that my hair consists of thirty-two corkscrews. I am alarmed. Shall I look like a Negress or a Golliwog after all this?'[48] In 1953 a London woman sued her hairdresser for damages after having a perm: Pleasance Refitt regarded herself as looking 'like a golliwog'.[49]

It was also said of men. In 1977 a newspaper headline referred to Kevin Keegan (1951-) as 'the golliwog that bites'. An employee of a Swaziland school wrote in 1910 to *The South African Pioneer* describing some of the boys who laboured in mines as golliwogs because their hair was some three to four inches in length and hung over their foreheads.[50] Forty years later Australian surfers adopted the 'Golliwog Special', otherwise known as the

*14. Ridiculing a new 'golliwog' hairstyle for women in 1916.*

'Freshwater Frizzle', a haircut which gave them the nickname 'The Short Hairs'.[51]

Some well-known men and women were singled out for comment. Albert Einstein was described as having 'the face of an inspired and saintly golliwog' while Bob Dylan, in 1972, was noted as having 'golliwog hair'. A few years earlier the Beatles were routinely called golliwogs and were even described as 'the four golliwogs from Liverpool'. Shirley MacLaine's performance in *The Apartment* resulted in her being termed 'an adorable golliwog in green lingerie and inky wig'. The press criticised Princess Margaret's change of hairstyle in 1957 on the grounds it made her look like a golliwog. The following year twenty-two-year-old Tommy Steele was called 'a fair-haired golliwog' and by another writer as exhibiting 'golliwog mop-shakes of his golden hair'. As late as 1979 Martin Shaw was termed the Bionic Golliwog because of his perm. Among many others, Eleanor Roosevelt, Salvador Dali, Cleo Laine, Rowan Atkinson and Frank Zappa were also said to look like golliwogs.[52]

Some references to golliwog hair were directed at those with dark skin and include a comment by British soldier in East Africa in 1928 ('our dusky servant had been looked upon as a very fine example of a living golliwog, so woolly had been his head with a shock of hair to eclipse anything we had ever seen'), Baden Powell's description of Aden in 1935 ('You meet all sorts of interesting races there – Arabs, Indians, Somalis alias *Fuzziwuzzis* because of their golliwog hair'), a British army officer's account of coolies in Borneo in 1947 ('A number wore battered porkpie hats, sometimes with the crown removed and their golliwog hair sticking through the top like a chimney sweep's brush') and a travelogue of Fiji in 1959 ('You will like the Fijians, with their distinctive golliwog hair and friendly smiles').[53]

To a much lesser extent, young women of the Beat generation who took up the black stockings 'craze' in the late 1950s were called 'Angry Young Golliwogs'; they reportedly completed 'the golliwog look' along with loose sweaters, smudgy eyes and bushy hairstyles. One man asked 'Why do girls want to make themselves appear so frightful?'[54]

### Financial imperative

The golliwogg was Upton's *Deus ex machina*, the sudden and unexpected resolution to what had seemed like an insoluble financial situation. Her father's death in 1889 had left his sixteen-year-old daughter financially insecure. Four years later the family returned to England and Upton's books provided much-needed income.[55] Of the golliwogg's development she explained:

> 'He was born of no deep, dark *intentions* nor was he the product of a decadent craving for ugliness on the part of his creator. He has simply walked side-by-side with me out of my own childhood... Tracing him back to as near the beginning as I can

*15. Topsy in 1899.*

> get, he came from an American Fair. Farther we cannot go and must fall back on the Topsy theory – *he growed*. He fell into our hands when we were children. In those days he was nameless.'[56]

Upton's 'Topsy theory' referenced a character in *Uncle Tom's Cabin* who answered a question about her own origins and lack of parents by concluding 'I expect I growed'. To *grow like Topsy* was once widely understood to mean to grow without planning or design. While it is certain that Upton's doll was her inspiration, in his growth she changed the parameters of his physical nature; golliwoggs misrepresented men, in the same way as teddy bears were not bears.

In the early 1900s Mrs Bertha Upton wrote to American friends of her family's news. An American writer, who was possibly ill-informed, recounted their history and offered a version with different details of the golliwogg's origins ('One Christmas a friend gave the littlest Upton girl a new doll, a queer, barbaric, hideous thing conceived by a savage brain. It became the studio pet and after many debates as to its name, was christened the Golliwogg') and the purpose of the stories ('they were kept to entertain juvenile callers'). She recounted the happy life that the Golliwogg had provided for the family:

> 'The Uptons now have a home in Paris where the family are hard at work in art schools. Graphic letters come to American friends telling of life there where the charming mother presides over a pleasant little apartment. The children are progressing finely, best of all the boy Desmond, who at twenty-one has carried off high honors. Around the Uptons gather, for kindly cheer and the comfort of a home atmosphere, scores of American art students. Mrs Upton's letters tell an interesting story of Sunday evening spreads when the tiny apartment is crowded to its very limit and where she has achieved the difficult task of making the tea table look American with the products of a Parisian market. And of course, in the place of honor in that cozy French home sits the mascot of the Upton family, the hideous, wabble-joined, staring Golliwog'.[57]

## Ugliness

Florence Upton was mindful of the widespread and repeated criticism golliwoggs received for lacking beauty. She said 'Yes, he was ugly, alas! And that has been the cry most often raised against him. But this was an unhappy accident.'[58] A writer noted in 1904 'there is no doll a child loves like a golliwogg, the little ones seem to love its very ugliness'.[59] A year later another commented they

*16. 'Beauty or Beast, which?', 1913, was printed with the verses 'childhood innocence & beauty, strange that it should have a doubt, torn between desire and duty, which to choose and which to flout. Shall it be the flaxen dolly, pink of cheek and blue of eye? She would rather kiss the Golly, but I cannot tell you why.'*

were 'about as ugly a beast as ever entered the great doll family. It is black and ugly as sin and yet the children take it to their infantile bosoms'.[60] In 1905 they were compared with a Sudanese doll which was:

> 'Interesting as a specimen of how the little fuzzy-wuzzies amuse themselves. It was black and ugly enough in all conscience though not quite so hideous as our own popular golliwogg dolls. But the fact that it is made principally of mud makes it too brittle to be of much practical use as a plaything.'[61]

Not every commentator felt Upton's character was unattractive. In 1895 one reviewer protested 'to an imaginative child the golliwogg will be a thing of beauty and a joy for ever'.[62]

In the late 1890s and early 1900s there was a vogue for toys which lacked stereotypical beauty. In 1913 they included a policeman whose red nose indicated drunkenness, 'a so-called puppy which is a mere abortion with distorted goggle eyes [and] weird animals which never were and we may devoutly hope never will [be]'. The following year the author of *The Education of Catholic Girls* commented that 'something radically wrong' had occurred in nurseries: she pointed to the 'perverse reign of the golliwog'. In 1913 a visitor assessing toy shops noted many were 'wildly grotesque' but none were more so than the golliwog.[63] At this time it was recalled that initially the doll had been laughed at but subsequently became 'all the rage': by 1912 it was claimed that golliwogs 'held their own' in the nursery.[64] In 1916 another commentator noted the choice with traditional dolls: there was the 'unmeaning prettiness of the waxen beauty' and the 'unmeaning ugliness of the golliwog'.[65] One writer compared their unpleasantness with that of gargoyles and thought medieval craftsmen 'took the same delight' in gargoyles as modern society did with a golliwog.[66]

In 1916 Haidee Wright (1867-1943), an English stage actress, argued that the golliwogg was responsible for what she termed the 'Cult of Ugliness'. She believed the initial enthusiasm of children subsequently spread to artists who created the first Post-Impressionist art, 'a gollywogg of wet paint', followed by writers who wrote on 'ugly themes'. Furthermore, she blamed the gollywog for women discussing, both privately and in public, 'ugly gollywogg subjects' such as physical intimacy:

> 'There was an avalanche of ugly toys. Musicians clamoured for dissonances; cubists clamoured for a relief from the round; poets rebelled against meter and rhyme. Girls clamoured for ugly, free lives and ugly, free loves; married women rebelled against their duties; they preached birth control; they objected to bearing children. Uncouth pets, eccentric dancing, flirtations with the occult – intellectual horrors; cabarets – silly games all of them!'

She predicted the ugliness cult would bring forth the Antichrist.[67]

In 1929 a specialist of mental diseases argued that golliwogs were unsafe for children and that they should be banned. Dr G. E. Mould urged:

> 'If children have as playthings such distorted objects as golliwogs, they are likely to get distorted views of life. But some dolls are as ugly as golliwogs. It is bad for children to be given ugly playthings. Why not accustom them to the beautiful by giving them beautiful things to play with? At the least, extreme ugliness in toys and dolls should be avoided.'

His list of 'mental dangers' comprised seances, bad films, noise and golliwogs. The previous year Sir George Clausen (1852-1944), a British artist, attributed the ugliness of modern art to children having been 'brought up on the golliwog'.[68] A few years later, in 1936, Dean William Inge (1860-1954) felt the figure was part of the 'decline of the West'. He wrote: 'There is hope that golliwogism in art may be a symptom of a fatal disease which will carry its victims into nothingness and oblivion. The aberration will then be looked upon with amazement, that is to say, if we recover from it'.[69]

In 1929 an American friend of Florence Upton was moved to defend her against charges that the golliwog was an improper toy. Henriette Lewis-Hind (1862-1938), believed:

> 'Those of us her friends, and they were many, not counting that vast troop of little children, her readers, hope with an abiding hope that Florence Upton's apotheosis was just an arising into light, as simple as a lark's rising into the sky singing. She wrote to one of those friends *We must have faith and fight on, and count it as something if we can make a little child laugh.* This Florence Kate Upton did, and she made them happy and taught them wholesome lessons'.[70]

The inferior character of the minstrel's personality differed from that of Upton's golliwogg who was adventurous and a loyal and intimate friend, if not foil, to the collection of Dutch female dolls. Shortly after their appearance the golliwogg was described by a journalist as a 'good-hearted, black-faced, big-eyed, bushy-headed gentleman'. In 1896 one reviewer described the 'swarthy, mop-headed doll' as 'amiable, brave and full of resource, though he is undoubtedly repulsive and terrifying in aspect'.[71] A Canadian reviewer in 1901 summed him up as 'a big black rag doll' who 'leads the others into mischief always, and perhaps there is a moral there, though Miss Upton kindly forgets to mention that.'[72]

It is significant that commentators at this time did not connect golliwoggs with minstrels. An exception was Angelo John Lewis (1839-1919), a prolific children's writer who in 1909, fourteen years after the character was created, felt compelled to ask and answer the question *What is a golliwog*? He explained it was: 'A doll of small size but fearsome aspect having an ebony complexion, black hair (a la Paderewski), goggle eyes intensely white and blubber lips intensely red. In dress he affects the modest fashions of the seaside *n*gger*.'[73]

*17. Ignacy Jan Paderewski, early 1900s, who was called a golliwog in 1909.*

In 1895 the golliwog eclipsed what had been the most prevalent Black image in Britain, the Wedgwood depiction of a kneeling slave in chains asking 'Am I Not A Man And A Brother?', which had been created in 1787. It continued to be in vogue until Emancipation in 1834 when it became redundant and was finally overtaken by the golliwogg in 1895. In 1900 a book reviewer in *Black and White* wrote that 'Someday the adventures of the Golliwogg may come to an end, but the Golliwog can never die'.[74]

*18. This Abolition medallion became Britian's most prevalent image of a Black man until it was supplanted by the golliwog, 1787.*

This first phase in the golliwogg's history witnessed its creation enthusiastic reception from children and adults. They recognised this fairyland character was unlike any other and found him engaging and loveable. Despite this, or because of it, he was constantly referred to as 'grotesque' and men and women with shaggy hair became known as golliwogs while modern art was described as being 'golliwog'.

# CHAPTER 3

# Appropriation

The popularity of Florence Upton's creation was not overlooked by other writers.

The golliwogg's appeal was rekindled between 1896 and 1909 when a new book of his adventures was issued for Christmas. However, Upton neglected to patent her golliwogg and it was appropriated by companies and other writers. In 1948 Edgar Osborne (1890-1978), the distinguished librarian and founder of an important collection of children's fiction, prophesied that golliwog dolls would overwhelm the memory of Upton's literary character.[75] His conclusions were well-founded: the golliwogg was overcome and vanquished by a tide of new fiction and commercial products dedicated to the golliwog.

## Enid Blyton, 1926-1986

The most prominent appropriator was Enid Blyton (1897-1968), the best-selling children's author. Her first golliwogs appeared in the 1920s and 1930s in such plays as *Magic Apple*, *The Toys That Came Alive* and *A Visit to Nursery-Rhyme Land*. In 1954 one critic commented on her *Noddy in Toyland*, which featured three golliwogs, that 'there can no longer be the slightest doubt that Enid Blyton knows just what to give the kiddies'.

She followed her plays with a number of books which had a golliwog as a central character. In 1935 she wrote *The Silly Golliwog and Other Stories* followed two years later by *The Tricky*

*19. Golliwogs were taken up outside Britain including in the United States where* Ducky Daddles' Party *was published in 1918. It featured two golliwogs who contrasted in appearance and personality with the character created by Florence Upton. In it 'who should arrive next but two funny Golliwogs who came from Scotland where all the Golliwogs live. They used to live in a shop in Edinburgh and sailed across the ocean before Ducky was hatched. Their names were Mac Donald and Mac Pherson and each was called Mac for short. This made it very confusing because every time anyone asked a question like* What time is it, Mac? *They both answered and then you had to explain which Mac you meant.'*

*Golliwog*. Unlike Upton's benevolent golliwogg, Blyton's golliwog was sometimes not only mischievous but occasionally a villain. Her variant has been called, amongst many things, inherently ambivalent and transgressive.[76]

To a modern reader the most striking aspect of Blyton's *The Three Golliwogs* (1944) are Golly, Woggy and N*gger, the main characters whose favourite song is 'Ten Little N*ggerboys'.[77]

Initially there was no criticism of her work but in 1955 a letter-writer in *Truth* questioned Blyton's responsibility in influencing children's racial prejudice. He was unsettled by her portrayal of the golliwog as a villain in the *Noddy* series:

> 'It is possible, of course, to be over-sensitive about these things, but at the same time I would suggest that it is not enough to be innocent of evil intentions. One would not, for instance, try to impose a ban on the manufacture and sale of golliwogs since children love them, they no doubt do more good than harm. But it behoves such people as Mrs Blyton, who evidently has some influence in the nursery, to avoid such coincidences as making the golliwog the villain.
>
> Lest she feel persecuted in this matter, I would point out that there are others who are perhaps more guilty of this kind of insensitivity. When I see prominently displayed a box of dates with the trademark *N*gger*, or a window-display in Lyons' Corner House of cake-walking minstrels, or an Idris advertisement depicting a *coon*, or a young woman who, thanks to Horlicks, is able to work *like a Black*, it occurs to me that such things must at least cause some pain to Negroes who see them, if they do not actually contribute to the perpetuation of a dated, insulting, stereotyped view of the Negro as someone who is of course cheerful and *always singing*, but at the same time feckless and irresponsible, good for nothing but to be a minstrel or a manual labourer.'[78]

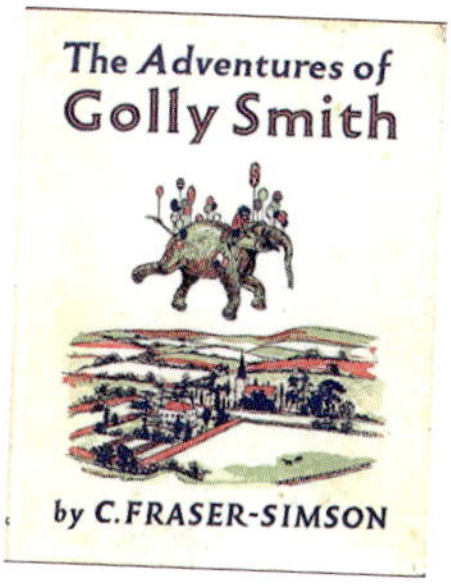


A London television critic suggested in 1957 that Blyton's choice of a golliwog as her scapegoat

*20-22. Three books which featured appropriated golliwogs.*

should have been avoided. He commented 'what an opportunity Miss Blyton has here of educating children to respect coloured people, if only she would care to use it.'[79] Her books began to fall out of fashion on literary grounds and met concerted opposition including being banned from city libraries such as Bury St Edmunds. Nottingham was another where a local resident concluded 'her characters are invariably mean, jealous, small-minded, boastful and, to use a local word, *mardy*'. She observed of *The Three Golliwogs*:

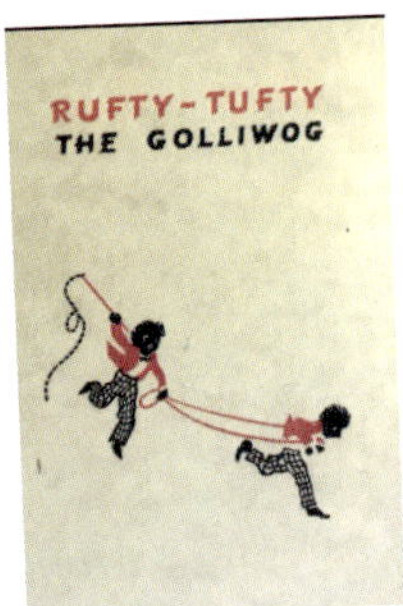


'The story was about Noddy going to *the dark, dark wood at midnight*. Noddy was very frightened. When he arrived at the wood, he was set upon by lots of black things that sprang at him out of the dark wood. I believe they were golliwogs. They stripped all Noddy's clothes off him and there was a horrible description of Noddy crawling out of the dark, dark wood on his hands and knees, quite naked, with tears rolling down his face.'[80]

In 1965, three years before Blyton's death she was criticised for her *The Little Black Doll* in which Sambo is unhappy until rain washes his black face pink. Blyton protested:

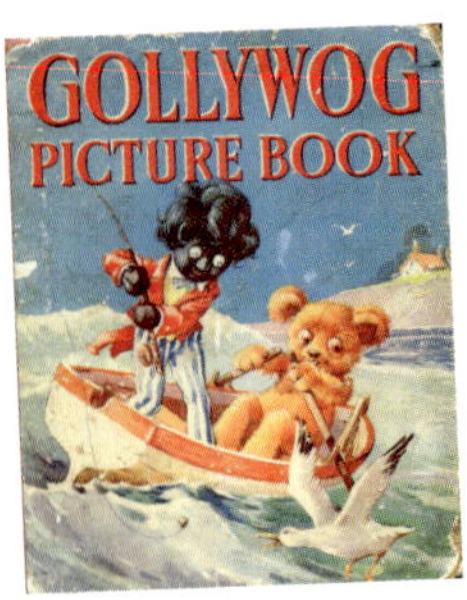


'I really can't remember writing anything like this at all. But I have written more than 300 books and lots of stories. I can't remember all. Besides, it ridiculous. Children love their black dolls and golliwogs. I have golliwogs myself. I adore them. It's fantastic to say that any child could have a

*23-25. Three books which featured appropriated golliwogs.*

colour prejudice about a doll or be made colour-conscious by this kind of story'.[81]

In 1971, three years after Blyton's death, publishers Purnell & Sons responded to a letter from the Race Relations Board regarding the offensive nature of the golliwog. Following discussion as to whether his skin colour should be changed to green, it transpired the correspondence was a hoax.[82] In 1972 Blyton's new editions continued to feature golliwogs despite what one commentator termed 'the hullabaloo about filling children's minds with racial prejudice'. Three years later, when an ITV programme featured Noddy but excluded golliwogs, the writer-producer explained 'I couldn't have written them in, they're too awful. The golliwog is a view of Black people which goes back to the Southern slaves. They had to go'.[83]

A seminal moment came in 1987 when the publishers replaced Blyton's golliwogs with teddy bears and monkeys. Gollytown was renamed Monkeytown and the bad characters were goblins. Initially, the official reason was commercial ('children today don't know what golliwogs are') but another spokesman subsequently explained: 'A decision was taken to take the golliwogs out. A lot of people feel uncomfortable about gollies either because they are felt to be racist or because they always seem to be villains.'[84] Ten years later the author of the first rigorous academic appraisal of Blyton's work questioned this widely-held premise that her golliwogs were 'habitually' naughty, if not evil and menacing. He concluded that other characters, notably bears, were more frequently associated with bad behaviour than the golliwog.[85]

## Other appropriators

An earlier appropriation appeared in 1901, 'The Gollywog and the Dutch Doll', a story entitled a 'rhythmic romance'. Over

*26. A Scottish golliwog from* The Chummy Book, *1924.*

the following years books about or with golliwogs included *The Adventures of Dumpy Dimple and His Dog!* (1908), *The Goblin Gobblers* (1910), *The Golliwog's Dreams* (1910), *Golliwog Stories* (1910), *The Golliwog News* (1913), *Wonder Book* (1913), *Where the Dolls Lived* (1919) and *The Adventures of Sabo* (1924).[86] Upton's death in 1922 left other writers a free hand in redefining the golliwogg in dozens of stories and books. Some even included Upton's Dutch dolls.[87] In 1904, *Dutch Doll Ditties*, was produced by Upton's own publisher. It omitted the Golliwogg who may have been replaced by Sambo but his features differed:

'Sambo was a Negro,
    Though not a Negro quite,
For though his face was very black,
    His body, it was white.

His hair, as well, was almost white,
    Which made the people scoff,
So he scrubbed his face with Binks's soap,
But his smile alone came off.'

*27. Another appropriated golliwog, from* The Adventures of Dumpy Dimple and His Dog!, *1908.*

The golliwog appeared on alarm clocks, banks, bronze figures, crockery, parasols, playing cards, puzzles and stationery and private individuals made golliwogs: in 1912 a journalist interviewed a London street craftsman whose golliwogs dangled from the end of a stick.

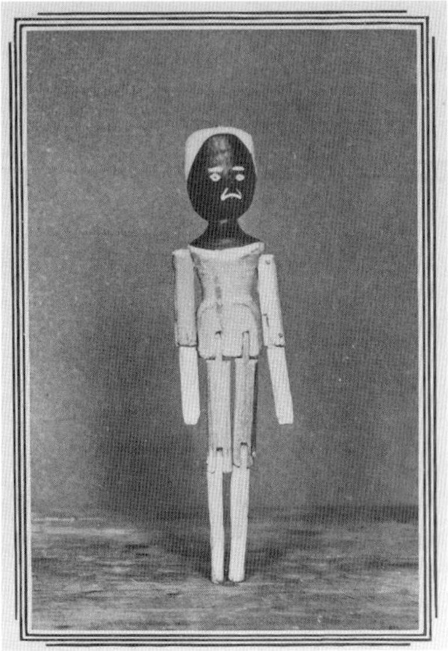

*28. Sambo in Louis Robbins' Dutch Doll Ditties, 1904.*

> 'Sometimes, sir, I sell no more than one in a day. You see, they're not everybody's choice and they are not penny toys. That makes all the difference. But, then again, I may have the good luck to get rid of a dozen, thought that's not often'.

Other products included a Royal Doulton bone china figurine of a boy with a golliwog and a disguised nightie case made of nylon velvet with a spotted bow tie and brass earrings.[88] From 1919 Vigny of Paris manufactured *Le Golliwogg*, a perfume with a 'bewitching' bottle-stopper. It was sold as 'the lucky little feller' and as 'the charming perfume in the bizarre bottle which is smiling on thousands of boudoir tables'. There was also face and talcum powder.[89] Once a week in 1924 the perfume was awarded

*Opposite from top left to right, 29a, English wind-up golliwog, c1935-40, which is missing the cane; 29b, a golliwog chair, c1960; 29c, Carlton Ware novelty porcelain teapot, date unknown; 29d, plate featuring the golliwogg and the Dutch dolls on their Polar adventure; 29e, paper doll postcard, early 1900s; 29f, Clarice Cliff bowl by Joan Shorter, undated; 29g, Crumpsall & Cardiff biscuit tin, undated.*

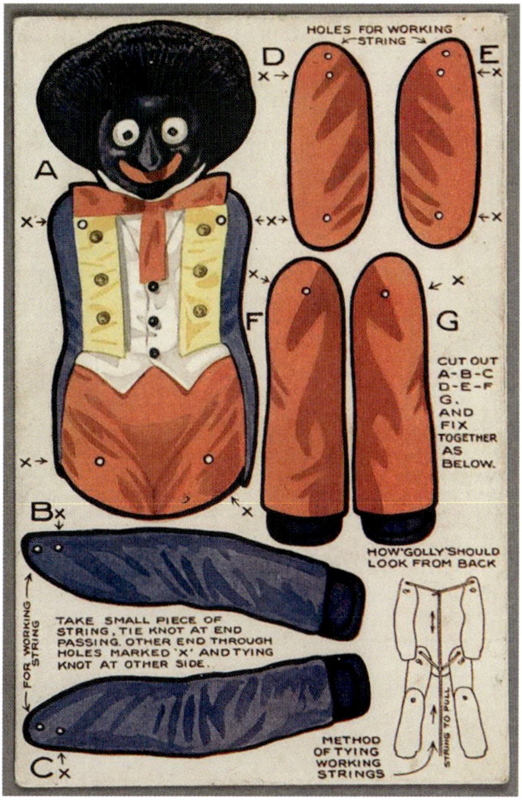
HOLES FOR WORKING STRING
A
B
C
D
E
F
G
CUT OUT A-B-C D-E-F G. AND FIX TOGETHER AS BELOW.
HOW 'GOLLY' SHOULD LOOK FROM BACK
FOR WORKING STRING
TAKE SMALL PIECE OF STRING, TIE KNOT AT END PASSING, OTHER END THROUGH HOLES MARKED 'X' AND TYING KNOT AT OTHER SIDE.
STRING TO PULL
METHOD OF TYING WORKING STRINGS

to a lucky couple at the Congo Room, the penthouse club at the Hotel Alamac in New York City, which was known for the 'weird devil dances' of Chief Sakabona Sonki and the illusion of 'cutting a live African slave in half'. That year an American firm also produced Golliwog Chewing Gum.[90]

The most popular items were the soft toys which were produced immediately upon the publication of Upton's first book. The golliwog's widespread appeal was recognised by a writer in 1927 who curiously noted 'the black-haired golliwog is the white-headed [especially favoured] boy of toydom'.[91] Many dolls were German-made which explains why, in 1915, a golliwog was executed in 'A Nursery Tragedy':

> 'Ah! A treacherous heart neath your bright crimson vest,
> And the words *Made in Germany* stamped on your chest,
> Have sealed your sad fate, and have doomed you to die,
> Golliwog, you were a spy.'[92]

In 1919 the 'New British Golliwog' appeared on a large canvas poster on a London building: dressed in a light red jacket, white waistcoat and light blue trousers, he was said to be an improvement on his pre-war German predecessor.[93]

The golliwog had various royal connections notably with James Robertson & Sons, the manufacturer which was given a Royal Warrant by George V in 1933 and subsequently by George VI and Elizabeth II. In 1996 a journalist asked a palace official for the monarch's views of the golly and was told 'Her Majesty never has her marmalade in a jar. She has it in a dish. But I think she might be broad-minded about gollywogs'.[94]

*30. Opposite page: Sixteen commercial and hand-made golliwog dolls.*

There were however many royal associations with the figure. In 1909 the favourite toy of five-year-old Alexei Nikolaevich, Tsarevich of Russia, was reportedly the golliwog given by Queen Alexandra.[95] During the war she was given another golliwog by a convalescent soldier. One of the favourite jokes of George V was:

> 'There was a little girl who wanted to take her doll to heaven. *Mummy, when I die, I want to take my dolly to heaven. Oh, I am afraid you can't do that dear. Well, then, may I take my old dolly? No, I am afraid not even that.* Whereupon, the little girl, losing all patience, said *Very well then, I will take my golliwog to hell.*'

In 1921 Edward, Prince of Wales, was presented at Blackpool with a golliwog made by a disabled former serviceman and purchased another at a bazaar at the Victoria Hospital for Children in Chelsea. A generation later a humorous writer noted that 'when Edward VIII did a Bad Thing, he became our black sheep too, but it was all right because it was a Royal Thing that he did, however negatively. He became naughty old golliwog, who has to sit apart from the other toys. But, deep down, we love him more than all the others'. Princess Elizabeth was given golliwogs at Christmas in 1926 and it was said two years later that one of them became a favourite toy; it was later called her 'prized possession'. Her mother, when Duchess of York, kept her own collection in her boudoir and was known to enjoy Upton's books. In 1932 Mary, Princess Royal and Countess of Harewood, visited the Children's Illustrated Book Exhibition and announced that the golliwog books in the Royal Nursery were among her favourites. In the 1930s Princess Elizabeth and her sister Margaret called Marcus Adams, the photographer, 'Mr Golliwog'. Shortly after the war ended four-year-old Prince William, son of Prince Henry, Duke of Gloucester, donated one of his favourite toys, his 'well-cherished golliwog', to sick children in Australia. In 1935 the Princess Royal purchased a sewing companion which was in the form of a 'golliwog housewife'. Twenty years later the Queen Mother bought a golliwog at the Commonwealth Exhibition in Marlborough House and two years later she found another for Princess Anne. Most recently, Camilla, Duchess of Cornwall, was seen to have attached a golliwog keyring to her handbag in 2008. One exception in the family may have been Princess Marina, Duchess of Kent, who banned golliwogs from her children's nursery because she felt they had a detrimental effect on mental health.[96] More recently, Princess Diana reportedly said that her two sons were not allowed to have golliwog dolls.[97]

In the early 1900s manufacturers and Upton's literary successors dropped the final 'g' in golliwogg, extended the figure's life and public visibility and fundamentally altered Upton's creation. They revamped the figure; it reverted to its original inspiration, Upton's childhood doll, as a human figure. The golliwog more accurately copied the American minstrel dandy's appearance and character. Whereas the golliwogg was consistently kind, gracious, joyful friend, the golliwog became occasionally spiteful, mean, loathsome and joyless. One commentator pointed out in 1971 that he had become a wicked villain 'symbolising the ingrained evil of his Black kind'.[98]

Robertson's first golliwog advert appeared in 1915 and other firms also used the character to promote products. For instance, in 1910 a Scottish firm advertised its Balmoral Cleanser with a drawing of a Black man, dressed in only white shorts and hat, saying 'Golly, it makes me and ma kilt terribul clean'. The soap turned 'black white'. A year earlier, in 1909, Sunlight Soap emphasised, by a girl holding a golliwog, customers would not receive 'black looks' if they used the product. 'Golly, you need it!'[99] Unlike Upton, some copyists deployed race not only in their

*31a and b. Two adverts featuring golliwogs and race, 1909 and 1910.*

visual representations but skin colour was pointedly referred to in advertisements. In this, commercial firms capitalised on the adult perception of the minstrel dandy as a figure of fun while at the same time they presented children with golliwogs who were friendly, welcoming and engaging characters.

Guest's embraced golliwogs with its Australian biscuit named Golliwog in 1912. The British version was made by Arnott's in the 1960s and was rebranded a generation later as 'Scalliwag'. Golliwogs promoted Glaxo Baby Milk in 1920, Toblerone in 1926, Rigmel in 1936, Persil in 1939 and the early 1940s, Rose's Lime Juice and Vinolia Baby Soap in 1946, Quality Street in the 1950s, Allinson's flour in 1950 and Cadbury's in 1954 let alone the fictitious Gumble's Golliwog Krisp Kurlers in 1925 and Golliwog Pickle in 1962. As late as 1962 Sunbeam produced a tricycle line called the Gay Golly; in 1980 it was renamed, for two reasons, the Baby Bunny.[100] In 1966 a golliwog advertised Inter-City travel on British Rail.[101]

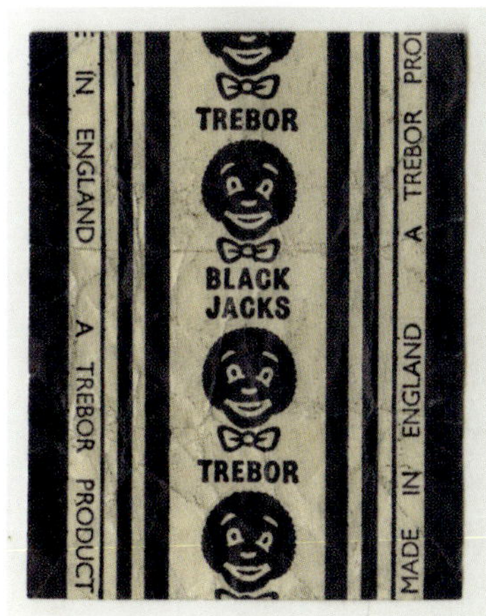


*32. Top: Guest's biscuits.*

*33. Above: Wrapper for Trebor Black Jacks, no date given.*

As the golliwog evolved into a closer representation of American minstrel dandies in the 1910s and 1920s, it later became identified with Caribbean immigrants in Britain. This replacement figure, particularly that created by Robertson's, has cemented the way in which modern Britain now

*34. Pinto 'the white-faced golliwog' in 1926.*

remembers golliwogs but many others were made by hand in wood, paper, cotton, wool, stockings, nylon, or cloth remnants. These were often less accomplished; clothing differed and was even optional. Sewing instructions of 1927 directed that old black and tan stockings were reused to make 'Red Indians, golliwogs and picaninnies' while yellow, cream and fawn stockings were for 'Japs and Chinese' and white or pinkish stockings were for European dolls.

Golliwogs, particularly those dolls which were not commercially-made, appeared in a variety of colours. As noted earlier, the consistent feature was voluminous hair which appeared in a wide range of colours such as in 1929 when children in a competition chose brown, yellow and pink amongst other colours. Skin colour also differed. In 1926 Pinto, 'the White Golliwog', appeared in *Pinto's Panto*:

> 'Pinto was no ordinary golliwog; his face and hands were not black but just as pink and white as yours are. In fact, he boasted that he had a close resemblance to the very first golliwog, who he claimed was a really handsome fellow'.

In this children's story the first golliwog was White but fell down a chimney and became 'as black as a sweep'. The first adult to see him was repulsed but her child 'would you believe it? when the best baby saw the golliwog he opened his arms and crowed with delight and he cried until they let him take the golliwog to bed with him, soot and all'.[102]

In 1922 it was fashionable for ladies' golliwogs to be coloured 'beech', described then as a new colour. They had seal-skin hair and clothing was Turkey red and white which suited 'admirably his African style of beauty'. In addition to the inclusion of yellow golliwogs in an Australian story of 1914, in 1961 yellow golliwogs were reportedly worn at an English girls' school to indicate their loss of virginity. It inspired the film *The Yellow Teddy Bears* (which was originally named *The Yellow Golliwog*).[103] The girls' story was reported at the World Forum on Syphilis in Washington in 1962 and it was suggested later that the yellow golliwogs were those produced by Robertson's.[104]

Hand-made golliwogs had varying sizes. Some produced for fundraising could be large such as the one made in Chelsea in 1969 which had legs four feet in length.[105] They were also a mere two inches in size. The sex of smaller dolls was indeterminate but the majority of the others were male. Many children had golliwog families or 'tribes'. Commercial golliwogs were most often male but as early as 1899 Mrs Golliwog had appeared along with family members Master Golliwog and Miss Golliwog. In 1951 the 'woolliwog' was manufactured; she was a 'lady golliwog with moving eyes and jointed legs' and she was joined in 1962 by Suzy Golliwog 'a girl golliwog, an old favourite in a new style. She has rolling eyes, wears a gay coloured dress with big bow at neck'.[106] Golliwogs were not often sold with names. An exception was Sambo, an Australian doll in the 1950s which was advertised as 'Santa's favourite golliwog' who was 'all dressed up in candy-striped pants, two-tone jacket'.[107]

The figure emerged more popular than any other of Upton's characters and in comparison, the Dutch dolls have an insignificant legacy. The golliwog's prevalence as a doll was eclipsed only by its near contemporary, the equally-benign teddy bear, but teddies as named characters only gradually succeeded as Rupert (1920), Winnie-the-Pooh (1925) and Paddington (1958).

The revamping of this British fairy-tale character produced a more accurate representation of the human form but one which was presented with greater racial exaggerations. During these years children's books often had other racialised characters, such as Little Black Sambo, which did not become favourite dolls or trademarks. Many American, Asian and European peoples were depicted in the public realm but it was the golliwog who triumphed. The early popularity of the golliwogg led to it being redeveloped by writers, performers and manufacturers and this second phase remade the figure in its lasting form.

# CHAPTER 4

# The Robertson's Golly, 1915-2002

The adoption of the golliwog by James Robertson & Sons, the manufacturer of jams and marmalade, was a pivotal moment in the history both of the golliwog and of the firm. The company redefined the golliwogg and the golly came to define the firm.

In the early 1900s Robertson's created a new golliwog, the golly. It significantly increased the figure's public visibility, lengthened its longevity and, perhaps most importantly, fundamentally redesigned its appearance. An unforeseen consequence was that four decades later the company became associated with racism.

Unravelling this long history is hampered by the apparent non-survival of the firm's archive of business papers. Robertson's was a family-owned business from its beginnings in 1865 but it was sold in 1981 and again in 1987, 2000, 2007 and 2012. The papers appear to have been lost: its current owner, Hain Celestial Group, has asserted that it does not own any of Robertson's historical papers. It is possible, if not likely, that the loss was caused by one or more of the changes in ownership.[108] The following account has been derived from a variety of other sources but, not surprisingly, it is incomplete. The archival loss is particularly problematic given Robertson's was prone to issuing fanciful accounts of its history.

The firm maintained that the golly was created in 1910 by John Robertson (1859-1937), the son of the company's founder

*This page and opposite: 35, 36, 37 and 38. Perhaps Robertson's earliest adverts featuring the golliwog, 4 February – 9 April 1915. The first lived up to its promise regarding cheerfulness while another introduced minstrels' language.*

James (1832-1914). Reportedly he travelled through rural parts of the United States and came across rag dolls which had been made from discarded remnants of cloth. They were being played with by Black children unable to say 'dolly' and instead said 'golly'. He returned to Scotland with one as a gift for his own child and realised its potential (he had 'found the plaything so appealing that he brought it home to become a magnet to child customers, as official trademark and mascot of the firm'). Parts of this narrative are clear fiction, such as the origin of the word 'golly' and discovery of the figure, but it may be true that a family member had visited North America where he purchased a doll. What was clearly imaginative was the claim that the firm created the character; as one journalist pointed out in 2001 'not to mince words, the jam-maker stole the Uptons' pretty invention and has never given them credit'.

The firm repeatedly claimed to have first patented the golly in 1910 but this may not have occurred until 1921 if not 1932. It also maintained that it began using the golly on its trade materials in 1910. It has not been possible to corroborate this date but Robertson's first golly advertisements began on 4 February 1915. It may not be insignificant that this came shortly after the death of the company's owner, James Robertson, on 5 October 1914. The use of the golliwog was a change in advertising strategy: in 1913 and 1914 the company had occasionally used 'The Golden Shred Factory Girl' to promote its products. There were various slogan campaigns in those two years ('Are bachelors lonely? Those who have Golden Shred Marmalade for breakfast say No! The fruit of happy solitude' and 'Every Irishman is an Orangeman when Golden Shred Marmalade for breakfast is the Home Rule'). In 1915 the company revamped its advertising campaign when it commenced golliwog advertisements. In one instance the figure was given 'Black' language.[109]

In 1961 the company projected another version of its history; the golliwog 'was dreamed up by an advertising agent'. Eight years

*39. Recipe leaflet featuring a golly, possibly 1940s.*

later the managing director claimed, with a marked degree of honesty, that a predecessor had concluded the jars needed a figure to amuse children: 'he thought of a teddy bear but golliwogs were fashionable then, so he used one'.[110]

An independent news story of 1943 credited artist John McDiarmid (1865-1942) with having created the trademark figure of 'a golliwog holding a pot of jam under its arm'.[111] The company had factories in Bristol, London, Paisley and Manchester where McDiarmid lived. He may have developed connections with Robertson's through its operations in nearby Droylsden. This would have been an updating of the golly image.

The firm used the figure not only on its jams and marmalades but on other products such as Golliberry, blackberry preserves, from the 1940s until at least the 1970s and Gollicrush, an orange drink sold in bottles, from 1958 through to the 1980s. In 1934 the golliwog had been touted as the company's 'ambassador'. Two years later the company's stand at the Grocers' and Allied Trades Exhibition at Manchester was described at length:

> 'Visitors may be mildly startled, that depends on their age, and they will certainly be amused by the representation of Ali Baba discovering Golden Shred marmalade. The door of the cave opens and golliwog brings forward a jar of the famous marmalade which puts the taste on toast. A golden light shines through the grand array of goods found in the cave and the attendants do homage to the great discovery'.

In 1951 Robertson's factory in Catford had a neon golliwog on its roofline. By then it was being said that the golly:

> 'Has become a national figure, a personage of importance, as well as being one of the best-known trade marks in the country. One thing is certain, he is sure of a job for life, as Robertson's would never dream of dispensing with his services'.[112]

Market research undertaken in 1961 confirmed that the golly was a 'very positive symbol' and that 'it is always associated with childhood memories and is very firmly linked with Robertson's products'. A respondent noted 'if the golliwog weren't on it, I'd say it would not be easily recognised'.[113] Robertson's became so firmly identified with golliwogs that newspaper headlines conflated the two such as '*Golliwog* standstill' in 1976 and 'Smile wiped off *Golliwog* group' in 1978. From the late 1950s through to the late 1970s the company was referred to as 'the golliwog firm'.[114]

Robertson's had a wide range and number of promotional products including, most notably, its brooches, badges and figures. The first was the 'golfing golly' produced in 1927. The linking of golf with a Black man was in itself mocking but it was very successful: the firm found itself initially unable to meet

*40. Collection of Robertson's badges*

public demand.[115] For seventy-five years Robertson's printed coupons on its jars which could be redeemed for golly items. This became the longest-lived corporate loyalty scheme.

Robertson's found diverse ways to promote its products. In 1935 it created Golliwog Pudding; a steamed dessert made of desiccated coconut, black treacle and Robertson's Mincemeat.[116] It was probably in the 1950s that the firm published *Detective Golly's Hand-Book with Some Hints for Young Sleuths*, a reimagining of the golliwog as a Black Sherlock Holmes. In 1955 a large mechanical golly was used by the Lincolnshire & Norfolk

*41. Christina Hewson, Robertson's 'Golly Girl' from 1971 to 1985, whose makeup required an hour's preparation.*

Dairies at a trade exhibition. Four female employees dressed as gollies.[117] The Robertson's figure became more visible when in the 1970s and 1980s golliwog hot air balloons became promotional features. Altogether there were four golly ballons (G-BBBT, G-BDFG, G-OLLI and G-OLLE). In 1973 'a golly girl, a perfect shapely replica of the Robertson's golly', rode in the wicker basket. The Golly Girl was Miss Christina Hewson who made promotional appearances including in opening a supermarket at Eastbourne where in 1973 'excited children and shoppers flocked to see Robertson's Golly Girl'.[118] She retired in 1985 and reflected that 'it has always been meant in fun - there was never any racialism in it'. Hewson added 'I've made more than 2,000 appearances during the past 14 years and never once was I accused of being racist'. Robertson's also had its own corporate plane, G-OLLY, from 1970 until 1988, with a golly painted on its tailfin.[119]

In 1976 the company sponsored Clare Francis (1946-), a former employee, in her transatlantic sailing in *Robertson's Golly*, a thirty-eight-foot yacht. Two years later the firm sponsored the golfer Nick Faldo (1957-).[120] There was also at least one instance of unwanted advertising: in 1967 Marmalade, a pop group from Paisley, used the golly as its symbol despite Robertson's objections.[121]

The golly's appeal amongst children cannot be overstated. 'Miranda', an emigrant to Australia, was probably speaking for many hundreds of thousands of former children when in 1936 she received a paper golliwog cut from a jar's label:

> 'As a little girl I was very fond of this marmalade. Silver Shred is the name of it and it is made in England. The most exciting thing about it was the black golliwog, one of which was stuck on the very jar. He was such a gay-looking little fellow and how pleased I was to see one again! I shall carefully keep him in my scrap book.'[122]

In 1980 Robertson's claimed that 100,000 applications were made that year for its badges, in 1993 6,000 badges a week were sent and at the end of the scheme, in 2001, the number had increased to some 250,000. Altogether it was estimated that Robertson's had supplied more than twenty million badges and in its last year, in 2001, some 60,000 people were registered with the firm as 'golly collectors'.[123]

*42. A Robertson's display board for mincemeat, mid 1900s.*

## Under pressure

The only acknowledgement the company has made as to the racial nature of the golly happened in 1962. That year James Robertston & Son identified it as a minstrel figure when it produced a twenty-minute industrial film, *Jam Session*. This promotional film was noted at the time as 'first-class entertainment'. Leading jazz musicians performed in the style of the late 1930s and the golly appeared in a production number based on a minstrel show.[124] This representation was not mentioned when the company was subsequently criticised by individuals and organisations including local councils.

The earliest concerted action against the golly took place on 29 April 1968 when a Ban-The-Golliwog campaign was initiated by Jeanne Langi (1934-2015), a thirty-one-year-old freelance journalist whose daughter was of mixed heritage. She stressed 'this lovable doll is a symbol of the White man's image of the Black man in the nineteenth century. The golliwog actually perpetuates the image of the Black man as a w*g and a funny creature. Each time a child sees a golliwog it is, in fact, a symbol of racialist bias'. Mrs Langi was interviewed by Bernard Braden (1916-1993), the presenter of a consumer affairs programme. The producer noted:

> 'White woman with African husband and half-caste child. After several years of working against racialism, has elected to concentrate on apparently trivial subjects which, she believes, cut deep. Campaign against Robertson's Jams *Golliwog* published in press this week. Mrs Langhi hoped that Robertson would elect to drop *golliwog* logo without pressure as good will gesture. Pointed out that they use kilted Scotsman in West Africa as Robertson logo there.'

A spokesman for the firm, P. T. W. Redsell, was also interviewed and the producer noted he was:

> 'Adamant in his views that golliwog not offensive to right-thinking people, and frankly concerned with economic advantages of this particular symbol and publicity scheme that accompanies it. Stated that Mrs Langhi had at no time approached the company to change logo and that company was unaware of her campaign prior to press reports. [He] did not see logo being dropped in foreseeable future.'[125]

Of the golly, Robertson's chairman asserted 'to suggest that it is a racialist symbol is utter nonsense'. A columnist with the *Telegraph* suggested Mrs Langi, a fellow journalist, had rediscovered 'an old standby on the humbler levels of the race relations industry' which caused offence to 'coloured immigrants'. She countered 'What I want people to do is to become aware that they're being indoctrinated'.[126]

Criticism of the golly was revived in 1972 when *Time Out* declared it insulting.[127] When, in the late 1970s and early 1980s the National Committee on Racism in Children's Books campaigned to ban the golliwog, the marketing manager for Robertson's responded 'the golly forms part of our national tradition and attacking it is an attack on a part of British culture'.[128] In 1984 and 1985 the Greater London Council threatened to boycott Robertson's products unless the golly was removed from its packaging.[129] Also in 1984, Merseyside County Council discussed removing Robertson's golly from the Jam Garden, the firm's trade exhibition at the International Garden Festival, because it was 'a prime example of institutionalised racism'. It relented when it transpired that the design was commissioned and created by the council's own Merseyside Development Commission. The scheme included a golliwog castle with nine 'giant-sized gollies' and 'extras in golliwog costumes parading the site'. Robertson's defended the golly:

*43. Advertising figure of a golly holding a jar of Golden Shred marmalade, undated.*

> 'Our golly is derived from an imaginary nursery-land character and has never been interpreted as anything other than a fictional doll. To draw connections between the golly and the Black community is, we believe, without foundation.'

Robertson's spokesman commented further:

> 'Quite frankly, we cannot understand the mentality behind their campaign. They say the golliwog is a racial insult. We ask politely and quietly *Please tell us why*. And they can't or won't tell us why.

> The golly started life as a doll. It is firmly fixed in the minds of children as a doll. The Stalinist suggestion that it is a racial insult is made only by a few White guilt-ridden liberals who see a caricature where none is intended, and who unfortunately believe that if they repeat the slander long enough, they will get their silly way. All they are doing is poisoning the minds of children to whom the golliwog is an object of joy and affection.'[130]

That year the Designer and Art Association awarded Robertson's a gold award for its festival poster 'on aesthetic grounds for the excellence of the artwork and the message conveyed by the post campaign'.[131]

Two years earlier there had been an increase in the sale of golliwog dolls and a Robertson's spokesman commented:

> 'I'm not surprised by their unending popularity. As a child's toy they are objects of love and affection. There are a minority who regard them as racial stereotypes and because w*g can be used as a term of racial abuse, we decided to abbreviate the name to golly. In 1980 there were moves to remove the golly from our label but the Commission for Racial Equality was forced to concede there was nothing illegal in it.'[132]

The firm maintained a Golliwog Productions Room at Droylsden in Greater Manchester. Letters were on display including:

> 'Dear Mr Robertson, on the radio we heard that some people don't like your golliwog because it makes fun of Black people. Me and Margaret are Black and we think it is very horrible for people to try and stop you having your nice golliwog on the jam jars.'[133]

However, in 1999 Robertson's admitted its symbol had an uncertain future:

> 'We have kept Golly under constant review for some time because of the way a minority feel about him… The sad thing

*44. Artwork for Robertson's advertisement, no date given.*

is that unlike so many modern children's characters, Golly is non-violent, positive and cheery. I can't see how he inspires racist language… But some people seem determined to see Golly as something he never was. It may be his time is coming to an end.'

Three years later, in 2002, shortly after Robertson's had issued a new set of badges, the figure was 'retired'. The official reason was that children no longer recognised the character or were interested in him. The brand director said 'We are not bowing to political correctness but like any great brand we have to move with the times'. Furthermore, the firm stressed the decision was made on economic grounds: 'While Golly still has a great deal of appeal among older users, he is not really as relevant as he used to be for

*45. Paper bag featuring Robertson's recipes, possibly 1940s.*

today's families. Children are not really interested in or familiar with the Golly character and we need to strengthen our appeal to modern families.' Upon its purchase in 2012, the new owner, the American company Hain Celestial, reportedly held meetings to discuss the 'totally toxic' historical association with the golly.[134]

The use of the golly by Robertson's for nearly the entire twentieth century gave the golliwog an extraordinary visibility and longevity. It is because of this that the racial nature of the golliwog was not adequately resolved but instead festered: despite the firm having had a series of owners, Robertson's has never accepted that its caricature of a caricature denigrated the Black race.

# CHAPTER 5

# Race

The public perception of the golliwog during the second half of the twentieth century was overwhelmed by racial considerations.

There were no race concerns about Upton's golliwogg but the revamped humanised golliwog has for some seventy years been constantly criticised for its physical attributes and for his altered personality. Racial undertones not only dominated its mid-twentieth-century history but the golliwog achieved the status of a racism icon.[135] This contrasts with protests Upton made in 1902 when she said 'The golliwogg *is* ugly but he has a good heart and he is a dear fellow and are not children way ahead of adults in reading character? They see his beautiful personality. What are *looks* to them?'

She created an admirable and respectable hero with 'dependable intelligence' as a fairytale character, a modification of her own doll which might not have been as readily accepted as her books' protagonist. Upton was either colour-blind or at least failed to anticipate that her figure would be seen as a Black man.[136] In regards to this, it is worth pondering whether the golliwogg's romance with Peg, one of the Dutch dolls, was intentionally bi-racial or had Upton disregarded race in respect to her characters?[137] A depiction of the golliwogg's children with Peg would seem to suggest that he was not considered to be Black. A few other writers also pursued golliwogs' romances with dolls or fairies.[138]

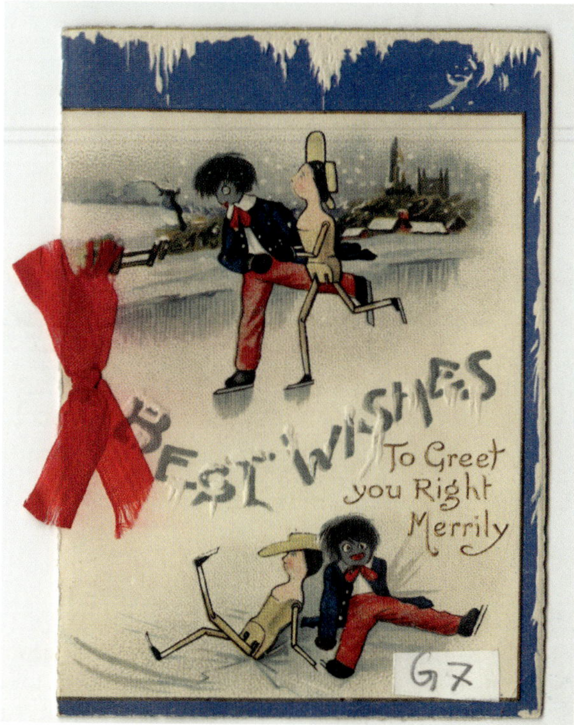


*46. A Christmas card with the Golliwogg and Peg, no date given.*

The character of the later golliwog varied whereas Upton was consistent in her thirteen books; her golliwogg was unfailingly inventive, kind, clever, bold, adventurous and gallant. She described him as a 'jolly dog', that is, a boon companion, and as 'a sincerity' and felt he had an 'honest personality'. In contrast, subsequent writers occasionally had him guilty of bad behaviour. In Blyton's *Here Comes Noddy Again* (1951) Noddy was car-jacked and stripped naked by golliwogs but did she imply they had sexually assaulted him as well?

Upton's golliwogg existed alongside a broader range of racially-inflected characters she deployed in her writing. Her *dramatis personae* extended to various Black and Brown men

*47. Postcard entitled 'Golliwogg Motoring', undated.*

and women who, in contrast, were identifiably human and dissimilar to the golliwogg. They included 'a jovial African with large admiring eyes', a highly-dressed banjo-playing minstrel named Sambo, 'red-skinned' Monday who was called a 'fuzzy-wuzz' and a number of cannibals. They were mostly depicted with exaggerated red lips and white eyes.

*48. The Golliwog and a Dutch doll promenading with their four children, undated.*

In *The Golliwogg at the Sea-Side* the group of dolls met a Black porter who spoke with an American Southern accent:

'What name, sah, did you please to say?
Is dis de right hotel?
De genman don't take foreigners
Unless dey're berry swell
Oh! You're de prince ob Golliwogg!
Den it must be jes so,
I'll take de ladies up de stairs
And show dem where to go'

He also had thick red lips, brown skin and his hair was more realistic for a Black man. In contrast, the golliwogg did not share his speech pattern.

Subsequent writers directly invoked the minstrel dandy not only by depicting the golliwog in human form but also gave him Black, rather than grey, skin.[139] Also, Upton's golliwogg varied his

*49. A Christmas card featuring the golliwogg meeting the hotel porter, c1898.*

*50. The cover of* Ten Little Gollywogs, *1909.*

clothing whereas the later golliwog wore finery. It was following this revamping that clear public identifications were made: performers called themselves the Golliwog Minstrel Troupe in Luton in 1915, the Golliwog Minstrels at Melton Mowbray in 1922 and the Golliwog Minstrel Party in Derby in 1924.[140] *Ten Little Gollywogs, a new story of the gollywogs*, one of the post-Upton adaptions, revised *Ten Little N*ggers*. This comprised readjusting illustrations of characters firmly into the minstrel tradition. In 1923 an observer of Christmas toys observed 'Golliwogs, both big and small of the negro or n*gger minstrel type, are chosen by many wee mites who seem to have a hankering after a black face and lemon-yellow-coloured hair.'[141]

Florence Upton's successors reflected late Victorian and Edwardian attitudes shown in *The Story of Little Black Sambo* (1899), *The Story of Little Black Mingo* (1901), *The Story of Little*

*Black Quasha* (1908) and *The Story of Little White Squibba* which was delayed in publication until 1968. Each was authored by Helen Bannerman (1862-1946) who had lived in India. Similar books by other writers include *Little Yellow Wang-lo* (1903) and *Little White Barbara* (1902) whose hero 'was called Little White Barbara because she had such a white face'.

It is reasonably assumed that most adults came to perceive golliwogs and gollies as Black men or black-faced minstrels. For instance, in 1927, a serialised children's story featured one character who addressed a golliwog as 'you old n*gger' while in a subsequent episode when the epithet was repeated the golliwog protested 'Me not n*gger'. In 1934 instructions on making a golliwog included the advice 'Don't forget to make the whole body of the golliwog black, because a n*gger is black all over'. Likewise, at Peterborough on New Year's Eve in 1953 a local man dressed as a first-footing golliwog in order to personify the 'black man who appeared at midnight to bring the traditional good luck'.[142] Many stories linked race such as 'Kenneth in Caveland' of 1919 in which one character was Golly the N*gger Boy while in 1940 a Lincoln charity sale had a golliwog labelled 'Sambo for luck'.[143]

Skin colour was addressed in a children's poem of 1920:

'Our golliwogs are two,
I don't know what they do,
Or why they're black
From front to back,
Like a sweep-jack,
Do you?'[144]

*51a-d. Christmas cards with golliwogs, early 1900s.*

Some meanings were ill-defined such as in 1940 when a thirty-two-year-old woman from Sudbury wrote:

> 'Really, Mr Golliwog, you're a funny fellow.
> Button eyes, striped coat, trousers bright yellow.
> When you try to brush your hair whatever do you do?
> I love you, Golly.
> But I'm glad I'm not like you'.[145]

What was presumably intended as an amusing story, 'A new kind of golliwog', appeared in a Canadian newspaper in 1930:

> 'The other day a kind lady took the minute, fuzzy-haired child of one of the Harmony Kings, a Negro quartet, to a big London shop to buy him a present, says Mr Gossip in the *Daily Sketch*. While she turned to talk to an assistant she left the child, rigid and wide-eyed with excitement, sitting on a chair among the dolls. When she turned round again, she was horrified to find a short-sighted old lady in consultation with another assistant. *What*, she was asking, "*is the price of this golliwog*? *It does not appear to be marked, madam*. Said the assistant, *I will go and inquire*.'[146]

In 1916 a nationally-serialised children's story told the tale of a golliwog who tried to change his skin colour:

> 'An unheard-of thing had happened. Golliwog had been invited to a party! Now, a party is usually a most joyful thing, and there is nearly as much pleasure in looking forward to it as in the actual party itself. And as this was to be Golliwog's very first party, he ought to have been nearly wild with delight. But instead of that he was just as miserable as he could be.
>
> The day before the party his friend Teddy Bear met him. *Gracious, Golly*! he said, *What ever is the matter? You aren't ill, are you? You look quite pale! At least no, I don't mean that, but not quite so black as usual. Don't I, really*? said Golliwog, and he brightened up wonderfully. *That's the best news I've heard for a*

*week*. Teddy looked at his friend sadly. *Poor old Golly,* he said, *you're going off your head, that's what's the matter with you*! *No, I'm not, Teddy, I assure you*, Golliwog replied. *But the fact is I've been invited to a party and I was so worried at the idea of being the only, er, black person there that I've been trying to wash the black off. The soap I've used, and the brushes I've worn out, you'll never believe! And my hair troubles me too. Every gentleman parts his hair when he goes to a party, and I simply can't part mine.*

*No*, said Teddy, trying to look wise and sorry at the same time. And then he began to laugh, and he laughed till be cried. *Excuse me, my dear Golly*, he said as soon as he could speak. *I'm awfully sorry, but I simply couldn't help it. Don't you see how silly you are? If you went to the party with a white face and sleek hair nobody would know you and it's you they want. If I were you, I shouldn't use any more soap. I should first give that dear old ugly face of yours a good polish with a dry cloth to make it shine; and I should go to the party as the Golliwog, with the mop of hair and the black face that everybody loves.*

*Really*? said Golly. *And truly* said Teddy. Golliwog took his friend's advice and enjoyed himself hugely. All the other guests were delighted to meet him and his joy was complete when, as he sat unseen in a dark corner for a few minutes' rest, he distinctly heard one of the guests remark to another *And have you seen our dear Golliwog? Isn't he perfectly sweet*? *Well, I never*! said Golliwog. *And think of the soap I wasted! And the brushes I wore out! What a pity! Oh, what a pity*!'[147]

More than fifty years later, in 1969, another story appeared in Children's Corner, a regular feature in the *Pontypridd Leader*. The golliwog was miserable because 'he wanted to be White with rosy cheeks like the dolls in the toy cupboard' but 'instead he was Black like a chimney sweep except that he couldn't even wash it off'. His solution was to cover himself with white makeup but it was removed because his owner, Ruth, said '*I do love him so, he*

"GOLLIWOG"
BRAND
FINEST SUPERCHARGED QUALITY
FLASHLIGHT FIRECRACKERS
頂靚電光响炮
MADE
IN CHINA
REGISTERED BRAND OF
YAN KEE FIRECRACKER MFG. CO.
HONGKONG and CANTON

Master Golliwog

Gollipop
COMPLETE WITH AIR POP-GUN

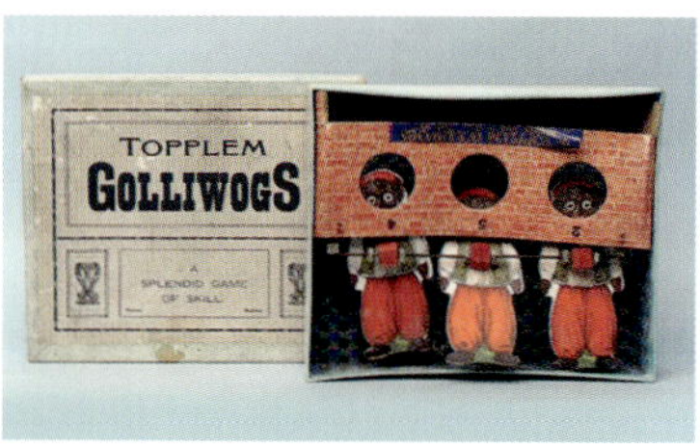
TOPPLEM
GOLLIWOGS
A
SPLENDID GAME
OF SKILL

*has such a dear little black face, quite different to my other toys. Well,* thought Golliwog, as he snuggled down in Ruth's bed that night, *Perhaps, it's better to be Black after all.*'[148]

In 1907 the *Westminster Gazette* ran an essay competition with the theme 'the Golliwog as a symbol of our national decadence'. In one submission the writer concluded:

> 'The black colour of this object is, to my mind, of the utmost significance. It was, I judge, a cynical acknowledgement of the failure of the White races in the struggle for supremacy and an admission that the future was in the hands of more virile people, savage and uncivilised though they might be.'[149]

The golliwog was a device to discuss the desirability of White or Black skin in 1913 when Meg Gehrts (1891-1966), a German film actress, visited Togoland in West Africa. She discovered that locals considered her deeply unattractive and was told by one boy 'you cannot help that. The good God made you so, did he not? We cannot all be black and beautiful.' Gehrts continued:

> 'Projecting my mind into theirs, and trying to think as they thought, I have come to the conclusion that they regarded me much as a White child regards a Black golliwog, as something to be frightened of at first, and yet cherished because of its strangeness and uncouthness. Only in their case the golliwog was alive, and so all the more fearsome until experience had shown them its harmlessness.'[150]

*Opposite page: Products from top left to right, 52a, the distinctive Le Golliwogg perfume bottle; 52b, Golliwog firecrackers, undated; 52c, a Master Golliwog, Jack-in-the-box squeak toy, wearing a felt outfit in a papered covered box, undated; 52d, a British 'splendid game of skill', Topplem golliwogs was similar to a coconut shy, c1920; 52e, Gollipop, an air pop-gun game, which differed from the Japanese record label and from Gollipops, the Trebor lollipop, undated.*

Gehrts believed the golliwog's appeal lay in its rarity. In 1908 'a schoolgirl' preferred them to White dolls and she explained in a national newspaper:

> 'I feel compelled to write a line in defence of the harmless golliwog. The good old-fashioned *golly* is certainly not good-looking, but not half so bad as it is made out. It has got, I will own, the *button eyes* but is quite cheerful to look at with its blue and scarlet hose. Among many families it is the preferred toy. Why the children's favourite wear-and-tear toys should be abolished for the flaxen-haired, breakable stranger I cannot understand.'[151]

In 1917 Sir Lionel Phillips (1855-1936), a South African financier and politician, made an unusual association following his visit to the French front. He had been tasked with monitoring recently-arrived troops from South Africa and observed:

> 'I would like to add that there is a tendency among some of the Tommies to regard the African native as a sort of golliwog, to be played with one moment and to be pummelled the next. The jovial-hearted Tommy expresses his benevolent feelings for his man as much in his punches as in his friendly advances, but the average African native fails to appreciate the loving kindness of Thomas Atkins in both instances at its full value'.[152]

The public's racial perception of the golliwog led to it becoming an abusive word. This was extended to some White men and women. For instance, when in 1934 Virginia Woolf (1882-1941) met the critic Cyril Connolly (1903-1974) she wrote 'There we spent one night, unfortunately with baboon Connolly & his gollywog slug wife Jean'.[153] More offensive was 'w*g' but it is uncertain when the term became derogatory. It may have been after 1922 when a children's story about the journey of Godfrey the Golliwog to the magic island of Wog was serialised nationally. However, by 1943 George Orwell thought that 'w*g' had become 'the most offensive of all the English nicknames for coloured people'. It then applied to dark-skinned people from Africa, the Middle East and Asia. In 1925 a British Air Force glossary for Iraq included 'w*gs, the people of the country'.

The word's origins have been disputed and there are usages for which no explanation has been found such as the Wog Wog Boating Club which met on the river Thames in the early 1900s. In the 1930s and 1940s it was occasionally suggested that w*g was one of five different acronyms. In 1936 it reportedly stood for 'Worthy Oriental Gentlemen' and in 1946 for 'Western Oriental Gentlemen'. Shortly before, in 1943, an Australian newspaper asked its readers 'How did the colloquial term *W*g* come to be applied by our troops to the Arabs?' One answer was 'From an alleged Army Order instructing the troops not to allude to these *Western Oriental Gentlemen* as *n*ggers*'. This explanation was disputed and instead w*g was claimed to refer to a species of water fowl. In 1948 it was suggested to have originated as 'Wily Oriental Gentlemen' but in 1933 yet another theory had appeared in a London newspaper:

> 'A w*g sounds a queer sort of creature. You naturally wonder whether it is a bird, beast or fish. But a w*g is a man, a native official of Iraq, and this name for all native officials in that country was coined by the British because they found that Iraqi officials had a habit of styling themselves *We Oriental Gentlemen*. The first letters of these words make up the slang name, *w*g*.'[154]

This confusion continued into the 1950s when a teacher of English explained to his students in Egypt that it was probably linked to golliwog but that 'there was a local, Middle East interpretation of the actual letters as meaning Wily or Westernized Oriental Gentlemen'.[155] It was also suggested in 1943

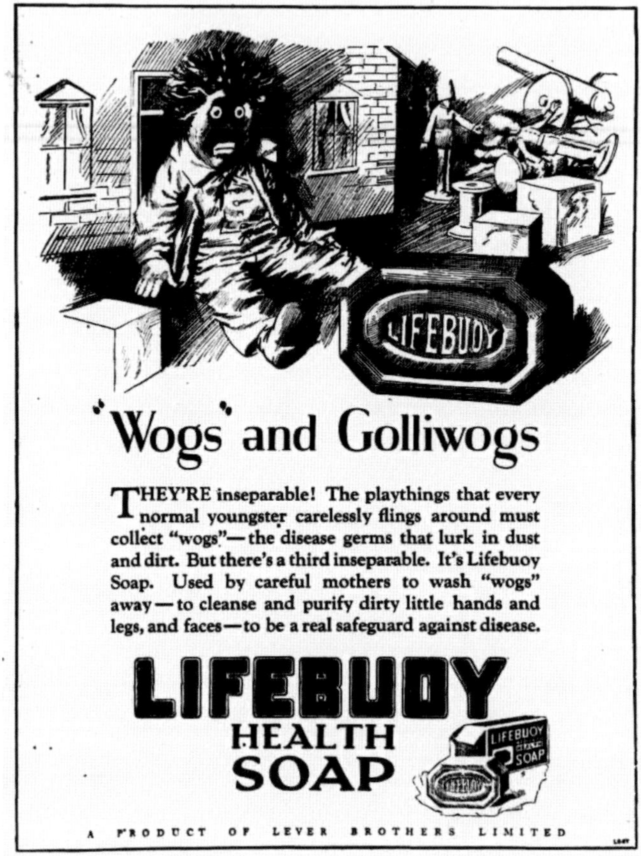


*53. Lifebuoy advert featuring an Australian definition of the word w*g and connection to golliwogs, 1930.*

that w*g was an acronym for Working on Government Service.[156]

These various theories attempted to explain a much earlier origin and by 1949 it encompassed all foreigners when a Labour MP archly said Winston Churchill (1874-1965) thought 'the w*gs start at Calais'.[157] It passed into common usage and was used in the early 1960s in Plymouth during a demonstration on the Hoe in Army Week when 'rioters dressed as Arabs' attacked soldiers. It was advertised as 'provoked by some of their own fellow-soldiers disguised as w*gs, who will shower them with abuse and missiles'.[158] In 1923 the Australians had a different definition; w*gs were 'germs of disease'.[159]

Another concurrent explanation is more plausible. In 1942 a British newspaper columnist noted it referred to West Africans and Egyptians and questioned whether servicemen had contracted 'golliwog'.[160] Instances of this can be found in Britain as early as 1916 when the storyline of *In Gollywog Land,* a British film, included 'six little *w*gs'* and in 1923 a children's story used Woggy as an abbreviated nickname for a golliwog.[161] 'W*g had been used as a nickname for Indians by 1921[162] when it was suggested that this was an abbreviated form of golliwog. A few years earlier a journalist recorded a 'camp of golliwogs' in Bagdad who comprised 'aborigines' brought in from Bengal:

> 'The full round cheeks of the little men made their black skin look as if it had been sewn up tightly and tucked under their chin. They were like happy golliwogs and the dust in their elfin locks, the colour of tow, increased the impish suggestion of the toyshop. The expression on their faces is singularly happy and innocent, and endorses everything Rousseau said about primitive comment. Evolution has spared them, they have even escaped the unkindness of war.'[163]

An interesting use of the word golliwog was made in 1930 by Churchill in his memoirs. In remembering his time on the border of Afghanistan and Pakistan in 1897, he equated Sikhs with golliwogs:

> 'I could only follow by fragments what happened after that. One of the two Sikhs helping to carry my wounded man who was shot through the calf. He shouted with pain; his turban fell off; and his long black hair streamed over his shoulders, a tragic golliwog. Two more men came from below and seized

Joyeux Noël
SANTA CLAUS ON HIS ROUNDS

TO WISH YOU A REAL JOLLY TIME THIS CHRISTMAS.
A Christmas very merry and bright
And plenty of gifts to bring you delight.

A CHRISTMAS GREETING
AND I'M SO SHY!
X X X X X

A Merry Christmas
Look what I've found in my stocking

> hold of our man. The new subaltern and I got the golliwog by the collar and dragged him along the ground. Luckily it was all downhill. Apparently, we hurt him so much on the sharp rocks that he asked to be let go alone.'[164]

The term evolved in 1932 with the 'n*ggerwo*g', a toy described as a friendly and cuddlesome little fellow whom any child would love to take to bed. His 'body is like a ball of wool and his head a smaller one, and his long thin arms and legs have enormous hands and feet.' There was a smaller version for car windows.[165]

### Two concurrent perspectives

Two divergent sets of perspectives reveal significant aspects of the historical background of the golliwog. One widely-held view, that of White former children, shares four common factors. A woman now seventy-seven-years-old recalls:

> 'The golly I had as a child was simply another soft toy. I wasn't told by my parents it was representative of a Black person and in any case growing up I don't remember knowing anyone who was Black, or that there was anyone in the schools I went to who was Black (or any other nationality for that matter).'

Another, now seventy-one-years old, has remembered:

> 'My golliwog was called Gilbert and was made by my great grandmother, he had a silk shirt, striped waistcoat, green tail-coat, striped trousers and a lovely smile. He slept on the bed with a teddy and two rabbits. He was a golliwog in the same way as my rabbits were rabbits. I had never considered him to represent a Black person.'

*54a-d. Opposite page: Christmas cards with golliwogs, early 1900s.*

Likewise, a seventy-year-old from Hertfordshire has reminisced:

> 'I had at least three gollies - knitted by my grandmother, so they were soft and cuddly. I believe Gran knitted gollies for all the little girls in our road and also gave them to charity bazaars. They were lovely! Gollies figured in Enid Blyton's books about Noddy and Big Ears - we had no idea they could become an insult. We used to play with a little Black boy called Peter who lived next door. He was real, the gollies were toys. We didn't associate the toys with him and his family. I expect we were naive (innocent).'

Yet another former child, now eighty-nine-years-old remembers:

> 'Everyone called the toys gollywogs. I don't think any of it was intentionally racist. I loved my golly and took him to bed every night. I was born in 1936 and my favourite author was Enid Blyton and her little stories with naughty golly. I loved him dearly. I don't think we thought of them as people, just dear friends in stories and on pots of jam. There was a huge amount going on with a massive world war looming, lots to worry about, with food shortages and bombs. People didn't have time to worry about racial questions. During the Second World War our village was flooded with Black American soldiers, who were segregated from the Whites. Waiting to be shipped to France, they were warmly welcomed even when it ended with two black babies where I lived with my grandmother. The one thing that later did worry me was the Black and White Minstrel Show on TV. I hated to see white men dressed up and blacked up in a mocking way.'

*55. Opposite page: Sixteen examples of commercial and hand-made golliwogs dolls.*

One eighty-two-year-old Exonian recalls:

> 'I was not lucky enough to personally own a golliwog but both of my daughters had one and really loved them as just another cuddly toy. Both were just called golly and sat at the end of their beds between teddy and panda. I also remember Robertson's paper gollies which were inserted in the labels of their jams and marmalades. We collected them to send for pottery models of gollies playing various musical instruments. We eventually had the full set which we proudly displayed on a wall unit just after we married. We never thought of them as anything other than cute little models and they were free!'

Another Exeter woman, now seventy-eight-years old, remembers 'I had a golliwog and loved it to bits. It didn't occur to me that Golly represented another race of people or even that it was Black. It was just another fun, soft toy to cuddle. I just knew I wanted one'. Similar memories are held by an eighty-five-year-old woman who was raised in Bristol:

> 'I was given a golliwog when I was three or four years of age. It was not new as the war was raging and new toys (and the money to buy them) were scarce. My golliwog was a soft toy made of black material (possibly blackout material). He had a striped knitted jumper, red trousers, and black wool for hair. He had been made by a friend of my aunt for her grandchild who had got tired of him and had moved on to China dolls. I loved him dearly but there was never any thought of race, he was just an addition to my collection of dolls. My golliwog was accepted without curiosity on my part.'

An eighty-four-year-old also recalls her childhood in Honiton:

> 'My doll is called Nigsie. The doll had belonged to my sister who had died a year before I was born. She came with her name. I don't know if the doll was new when my sister had it but she was born in 1933. I did have a cloth golliwog doll as well, called

*56. Australian campaigning artwork, c2010.*

Golly, but it disintegrated many years ago. She was accompanied by two teddy bears, a China doll with oriental features and two China-faced dolls made in Germany and France.

As a child I wasn't aware of the significance of the dolls. I am sure my mother wasn't either. Mother's best friend was a lady who had many Negro features, strangely called Miss White (which always amused me). It was never discussed.

When I was a toddler, we met the American GIs as we walked around our country lanes. They were billeted near us in Honiton, prior to the D Day invasion. I well remember some of them were the first dark-skinned people I had seen. My parents spoke to all of them as we passed by. I didn't think that it was anything unusual as their colour wasn't mentioned.'

Each of these independent memories shares not only a deep love for their doll but a disconnection of golliwogs from Black men and unawareness of racial stereotyping. Just as important is a fourth unrecognised factor; this generation takes for granted their youthful seclusion. It is not easy for modern society, which has been fundamentally altered by the rise and dominance of personal computers, the internet and mobile telephones in the 1990s and early 2000s, to understand the isolated world of children raised in the 1940s, 1950s and 1960s. That generation's transformative change was the creation of ITV in 1955 and BBC2 in 1964 and it fails to engage with recent technological advances to the same degree as the younger generation. Their exposure to the wider world was then, and remains today, profoundly different.

Another factor needs to be considered: the older generation of these children lived through the zenith of the British Empire. Not only did children celebrate Empire Day on May 24 but they had lessons in school that the British were superior as a race and had a divine obligation to maintain its empire. It would be illogical to ignore the effects of four centuries of colonisation upon the perceptions of two hundred million subjected people, particularly of those who came from the West Indies whose ancestors were enslaved. To what degree were these unintentional views of members of colonial races deeply-engrained and pervasive or were they removed from everyday life in rural counties?

A contrasting view of golliwogs is held by some Black men and women. Typical of the associations recognised by middle-aged Black British men and women are those of an Exonian, now fifty-nine-years-old and who was raised in London; he recognised them as 'crude stereotypes of people of African descent'. A Barbadian woman who came to Britain as a child in 1961 recalled:

> 'My daughter she went to an all-White girls' grammar school and I had to do what a mother had to do to protect my daughter in the sense that I had to speak out for her. I never went to the teachers because they used to write notes and call her black pig and gollywog and [asked] *Why don't you go swing in the trees*?'

She spoke to the other girls:

> 'I said *I am Pauline's mum* and I said *You've been calling her*

> *names and telling her she's a gollywog and this and this.* I said *Why you doing this*? They said *We don't like her as she's the only one in school.* So I says *OK.* I says *This is your blouse*, cause they were wearing nice navy and white. I say *This blouse is white, isn't it*? She says *Yes*. I said *What's the colour of your skin?* She says *Um, pinky, pink, a sort of pink.* I says *OK, you got a cat at home*? She says *Yes*. I say *You got a dog*. She says, *Yes*. I said *When you go home you take your hand and you pull away the hair of the dog or skin of the cat and that's the colour of your skin*. And I say *You say her hair is woolly like a gollywog*. I says *Have you seen the horse's hair?* She says *Yes, the tail.* I say *That's what your hair is like*. And I said *You said she got a nose, a big, flat, black nose.* I said *Have you seen the fowl's beak*? I said *That's what your nose is like*. But some people might say I was racist in doing that to children, to say that to a child, but I did that to make people realise you can always find something about someone that will make them feel bad'.[166]

Likewise, Bev Provost, who as a five-year-old came from the Caribbean to Brixton in about 1950, said in 1977 'I'm still burning with bitterness at what happened. I was spat on and abused. They kept asking me, *Golliwog, where's your tail*?'[167] Equally severe were the experiences of Michael Baptiste, an NHS employee, who recently wrote:

> 'I have been a mental health nurse for more than 25 years and have been on the receiving end of racism from patients my entire career. Patients have called me racially abusive names such as black gorilla, n*gger, black Sambo, golliwog, monkey, Chicken George, and I have been told *Go back to your own country*. It is an issue that refuses to go away.'[168]

Salman Rushdie has recalled his distress at being called a w*g as a thirteen-year-old schoolboy. He discovered a fellow student writing 'w*gs go home' on a wall and the moment he considers pivotal in his life. He also wrote 'Can there be another language with so wide-ranging a vocabulary of racist denigration… Yes, the golliwog, too; at football grounds, black players are taunted with the cry, *Get back on your jam jar.*'[169] Nearly the same words were spoken to novelist Esther Lawson as a child.[170]

Joe Allen, who emigrated from the former British colony Montserrat in about 1959, remembered in 1995:

> 'My sister and I started school almost immediately in Finsbury Park. As the only Black children we were called the golliwogs and teased unmercifully. When I told my mum about it, she asked me how I handled it. I told her *the other kids laugh, so I laugh too*. She said *Quite right, you go on laughing boy*, so I did and it seemed to work out okay'.[171]

Olympian Tessa Sanderson (1956-) has recalled that at school 'the abuse was stuff like *Hey, n*gger! I'm talking to you, blacky*. Guys would call me things like coon and golliwog. In those days golliwogs were on the jam jars and we Black kids hated them.' Perhaps the last highly-publicised incident involved Naomi Campbell (1970-), the model, at Heathrow Airport in 2008. She explained, in what was a contested account of events, 'I was called a golliwog supermodel. I don't think that's really fair, do you?'[172] What could be excused as unintentional or unconscious racism for some, was experienced very differently by others.

Perhaps the difficulty in untangling loaded language in regards to golliwogs is neatly exemplified in an incident in 1928 involving Learie Constantine, the Trinidadian cricketer, at Lord's. He received fervent adulation from one journalist ('that genius, that eye, that lightning judgment and wrist of wire') who described him as 'Black Magic' as well as 'this smiling darky'. After the match Constantine was surrounded by adoring fans and held aloft a black golliwog, 'the living spit of the wizard himself'.[173]

*57. In 1923 J. A. Bentham named his golliwog character 'Woggy' in his book entitled* Shoes.

Children in the first half of the twentieth-century continued to adore their golliwogs unaware of racial associations while simultaneously immigrants from the empire's colonies in the 1950s and 1960s were denigrated as golliwogs and w*gs. Racial considerations came to redefine the golly and golliwog. Amongst different sections of the public they were, at the same time, either precious or unpalatable. The validity of their feelings is borne out by former children, now in their senior years, being unable to discard their cherished dolls while for others the word golliwog brings back ugly memories of hate speech.

CHAPTER 6

# Golliwogs abroad

Golliwogs were known on the Continent and in the United States but were most popular in the British Empire, particularly in Australasia.

Dolls were sold on the Continent in Germany, France, Italy and probably other countries. In 1919 the *Cologne Post*, a newspaper published for the British Army of the Rhine, advised military wives on how to make a golliwog doll.[174] Thousands were sent to France during the Great War and it was there that the golliwog perfume was created in 1919. That year it was said that 'Paris has startled everybody with her new coiffure. It is that of the golliwog, as bushy as possible'. The French adapted the word. In 1923 men from their colony of Senegal were called golliwogs. In 1945 General Charles de Gaulle (1890-1970) reportedly describes three North African leaders as the 'Golliwog Kings'.[175] The French had their own versions during the Great War: Nenette and Rintintin were popular yarn dolls. These 'Paris golliwog charms against air raids' were even occasionally available in England such as on 19 July 1918 which was celebrated as 'France Day' in Exeter.[176]

## The United States

Golliwog dolls were commercially available in the United States and Upton's books were favourably reviewed in leading newspapers but the character does not appear to have been popular. Scattered references can be found such as in 1912 when 'golliwog comic darkey figures' could be purchased in New York and that year a San Francisco bookshop tried to drum up

# Iceberg Mystery Explained

## Strange Creatures Are Gollywogs

## Can Be Seen Today at Wanamaker's

It is marvelous! It is unbelievable; it is—but, there; you will hear what was told us by Mr. Elgnirk Ssirk himself. He arrived at the store last night—this Elgnirk Ssirk. With him were his wife—our Sitka correspondent—and their curious charges.

### Elgnirk Ssirk—Kriss Kringle

Have you spelled Elgnirk Ssirk backward? We have; we did it last night. Then we said, "Hello, Kriss; you jolly old tease—you've had Philadelphia wild with curiosity."

"That's good," he replied; "we'll have the merriest Christmas squatdoodle in years."

"Squatoodle, what's that?"

"Why squatoodle in Icelandic means a six weeks' party."

### What Gollywogs Are

"Speaking of Iceland," he continued, "I have determined the species of our guests. They belonged to a race that lived 5000 years ago. A bitribal colony in the North. One faction was called the Gollies (later perversion being Gauls), the other faction called themselves Wogs. Combining the two we have Gollywog."

"But how do you account for their sleep of 5000 years? How do you explain their costume, which is of an emphatic modern cut?"

Kriss smiled. "It seems," he said, "that one day, 5000 years ago, the gulf barrier burst. Millions of tons of water swept their city. All the inhabitants save those that are here were killed. The rest were swept to the Ultarctic Sea. There the cold descended suddenly, like a knife.

"The heat and chemical attraction of the Gollywogs caused a local gravitation of water, encasing each in an iceberg. So instantaneous was the freezing that only the epidermis was congealed, the reaction stimulating the motion of the interior human machinery. In short, our Gollywogs have been INTERNALLY ALIVE AND EXTERNALLY DEAD FOR 5000 YEARS!"

### Fashion Moves in a Circle

"The modern clothes? Why, fashion comes and goes hundreds of times in 5000 years! A decade hence the Mayor of your city will, like as not, be wearing sandals and a toga."

"As for the Gollywogs themselves," said Kriss, "it is natural that a race antedating all anthropological records should possess undeveloped intellects. Result—these queer folk, despite their mature age, are congenial companions for none but children. Being desirous of introducing them where they will meet the largest number of children, my good wife and I brought them to Wanamaker's.

### In Arms of the Polar Bears

"Evolution was in its infancy when our visitors formerly lived. Result—affinity between animal and man. Considering this, we sent you some polar bears a week ago to look after them."

THIS, children, is the solution of the iceberg mystery. In looking about for something new to bring to Wanamaker's this Christmas Kriss Kringle unexpectedly found the strange creatures in the icebergs. Then he had his wife, Mrs. Kriss Kringle, write to the editor of the Wanamaker page the stories you have been reading—just to mystify you a bit and get your closest attention.

*58. The gollywogs of Iceland, 1904.*

*59. Golliwog hearth brush, with horse hair bristles, manufactured by Biltmore Industries.*

business by installing a 'Golliwog Window' in which were placed 'real English Golliwogs'. They had been made by hand in the children's book room.[177] In 1965 a British toy manufacturer admitted the dolls' skin colour had made them unpopular amongst Americans. Dean's Rag Books Ltd introduced a new white-faced ragdoll, Mr Smith, because the firm had failed to sell a golliwog in the United States during the previous sixty-two years. A director explained 'Fear of offending people at a time when color is such a delicate subject has been the main reason why the golliwogs never made it in America, so what we had to do was make them acceptable.' It may have been to disavow any connection between golliwogs and minstrels that the company's representative claimed that the figure's history was obscure but he understood the name had first been given to black-faced dolls sent to England by British soldiers serving in South Africa in the late 1890s and early 1900s.[178]

The golliwog's rarity may have been caused in part by it having been registered as a trademark in 1917 but Americans may not have been charmed by a figure with a recognisable cultural background. They already had Mammy, a female version of a minstrel. In 1882, thirteen years before the golliwog was created, an American children's story featured Mary Anne, a 'very black doll', was serialised in newspapers. She was 'very popular in society' despite having exaggerated white eyes and red lips. Moreover, 'she looked so jolly that it made one laugh only to see her'. A string enabled her to dance but:

> 'it was not a dance suited to polite society that she danced – it was a real Negro break-down. Indeed, I do not think that nature had intended Mary Ann for polite society, but for all that she was very popular in it'.[179]

After Upton's death in 1922 her golliwog doll was identified by a Connecticut writer as 'a n*gger doll', a perception which may have been commonplace. In 1904 a Philadelphia store bizarrely introduced golliwogs as strange creatures whom Kris Kringle had found asleep in an Icelandic iceberg.

Despite their relative obscurity, curious applications of the word can be found such as the Golliwog Hearth Brush and Bellows which were manufactured in California in 1915. They were 'most amusing' as well as useful.[180] Golliwogs occasionally appeared on stage. In 1930, only weeks following the Stock Market Crash, the programme at a Baltimore theatre included:

> 'This attraction opened with a Golliwog back drop and the Chester Hale Girls came on in Golliwog costumes and masks hidden behind stage pieces designed like large jars only their heads visible. They came out of the jars and went into a routine dance with music by the band behind the back drop. They sat on the floor and went into a tom-tom drill with a dance movement… Wesley Eddy was led on stage by four girls. He was dressed as a Golliwog'.[181]

In 1928 the Lime Brothers appeared on stage in Omaha in 1928:

*60. The Laverne interior design golliwogs, early 1960s.*

'*That act alone is a show in itself* says one of the dramatic critics of the city about the act of the Lime brothers and their Golliwog at the Riviera stage show. The Golliwog appears limp and lifeless, carried on the stage by the Lime brothers and tossed about like one of the long-legged, dangling French dolls. He appeared jointless. Finally, he was hung up on a leg and wound up and puts on a dance like an automation. Whoever he was who was masked behind the grotesque face of the Golliwog, he was a talented contortionist and actor'.[182]

In 1934 *Newsweek* referred to the Speaker of the House of Representatives as having 'an extraordinarily rampant golliwog mop of white hair' but other linkages did not necessarily indicate actual familiarity with golliwogs. In the 1920s and 1930s there were 'Golliwog' bridge clubs in such cities as Cleveland, Pittsburgh and Philadelphia and by 1919 Americans had even concocted a recipe for 'Golliwogs', a type of fried dough which differed markedly from the later British biscuits of that name. The Gollywog Tearoom operated in Detroit in the 1920s which may also have been the Golliwog, 'an informal restaurant in the Parisienne Manner', which was open by 1926.[183]

*61. A Golliwog Girl from the Golliwog Lounge, 1963.*

In 1924 Gloria Swanson, the glamorous film star, was captured in verse:

'Bobbed hair and permanent waves;
Wild music and tangoes;
Trailing gowns, Spanish heels.
Bizarre grotesques;
Golliwog perfumes;
Gaily-colored bits of Georgette;
Expensive jewels;
Wrecked automobiles;
House parties, proms, tea dances
And the never-ending whirl of life.'[184]

Eighteen years later, another Hollywood actress, Bette Davis (1908-1989), received on her thirty-fourth birthday small hand-made woollen golliwogs and dressed, for her 70th birthday, in black face and what was described by one guest as 'a golliwog wig'. Marlene Dietrich (1901-1992) kept a golliwog as a mascot. She brought it from Germany and it appeared in her first Hollywood film, *Morocco,* in 1930.[185]

In 1961 Erwine and Estelle Laverne, noted New York furniture designers, created Golliwogs, a 'tall, whimsical sculpture shaped like several hourglasses piled on top of one another' with a 'giddy' or 'colorful' male face over whose head 'you can find flowers, plants, fruit or anything you may wish'. Amongst other outlets, they were sold in Cincinnati where there was also Camp Golliwog for children in 1970 as well as a line of girl's suede shoes, called Golliwog, three years later.[186] New frames for eye-glasses, called 'the golliwog', were unveiled in 1967.[187] Perhaps the greatest indication that Americans had lost any cultural memory of the golliwog concerns a group of Connecticut schools. In 1999 children found a rag doll tagged 'golliwog doll' and made fifty copies for distribution in an elderly care home. They had no understanding of its historical background and decided the golliwog's purpose was to spread love, happiness and good wishes. After being told the doll was racist one teacher's opinion was that golliwog 'is a silly name. It means nothing more than a nonsense name that now stands for giving something to someone else'.[188]

Likewise, in 1962 a leading hotel chain opened Golliwog Lounges. The Sheraton Hotel in Pittsburgh established the nightclub as part of a scheme to give the new hotel 'loads of personality'. In this vein, its other public rooms were the Kon Tiki, the Cheshire Cheese and the Café Bonaparte. The lounge had the 'lissom' Golliwog Girls who were compared to the

Playboy 'Bunny Girls'. Two years later, the company placed adverts asking 'Why does the Golliwog Lounge have such a goofy name?' It refuted the suggestion that it was named after 'whimsical fantasy creatures' and instead invented its inspiration as Foster T. Golliwog, 'a noted *bon vivant* who came to an untimely end when he was trampled to death on a burlesque runway'. There were also Golliwog Lounges in other Sheraton Hotels in Chicago, Minneapolis, New York and Oklahoma City as well as in Toronto and Niagara Falls.[189] The lounges differed in character from the Golliwog Club, the Canal Street venue in New Orleans.[190]

Ignorance of golliwogs was furthered when in 1966 the British publishers of Upton's golliwogg books could not find an American publishing partner for reprinting the series. One reason was 'the colour problem'.[191]

**The British Empire**

The golliwog was better-known across the British Empire. Some sporadic references can be found including a traveller in 1901 who described watching in Baluchistan (Pakistan) a *Chota Sahib*, a junior officer, engrossed in *The Golliwogg in War*.[192] Upton's books were on sale in Canada where a reviewer in 1901 explained that the golliwogg was 'a big, black rag doll whom the Dutch dolls followed without question in innovative adventures involving bicycles, polar discovery and an auto-cart'.[193] It was claimed in 1909 that golliwog dolls had become popular in India amongst young girls although they preferred 'fair English dolls with blue eyes and flaxen hair'.[194]

Other colonies where golliwogs were sold include Rhodesia (Zimbabwe) by 1906 and at Gweru minerals were mined at the Gollywog Mine by 1914. In South Africa a range of golliwog

*62. The reach of the empire: a display of Robertson's products in a shop window in Lagos, Nigeria, 1952.*

products, 'laughter-provoking with its queer groups of black-faced porcupine-haired figures', were on sale by 1905. A few years later golliwog and suffragette brooches were on offer, along with 'Chinese slave bangles', in Johannesburg. In 1912 specifications for a competition for teenage girls excluded any mention of race:

> 'A golliwog, it may be as well to explain, is a rag doll with a fuzzy head of hair and goggle eyes. It must not be too pretty and is generally dressed in bright-coloured clothes. Pictures of golliwogs are to be found in most children's books'.[195]

As in Britain, golliwogs were popular in South African theatrical entertainment including comic dances performed by Miss Vera Kleudgen in 1910; she had been 'splendidly got up as a golliwog, did a golliwog dance, all the grotesque attitudes of the nursery favourite being cleverly executed'.[196] Golliwogs were sufficiently known in South Africa for a White cabinet minister to say to a fellow M. P. in 1995 'Don't jump up and down like a golliwog'. In his subsequent apology Pik Botha confessed to his

*63. The 'Golliwog Girl' in the postcard series Australian War Girls, c1914-1918, holding one of the now-forgotten incarnations of the golliwog.*

Black colleague that he had confused nursery characters: 'It was a jack-in-the-box that I had in mind'.[197]

## Australasia

Golliwogs were probably most popular in Australasia where a writer in 1961 described them as 'that fuzzy-headed nursery favourite with laughing eyes twinkling from a black face'. Some were individually taken to Australia, such as one clutched by five-year-old Sylvia Steer on the deck of a Liverpool passenger ship sailing to Australia in 1950. A writer observed a year before the creation of the golliwog that Black or mixed-race girls in Australia preferred to play with White dolls despite the prevalence of Black dolls in the shops ('the reason for it is of course a very pathetic

*64. Francis and Nea Birtles, 1935. Francis (1881-1941), an adventurer and traveller, died six years after his marriage on 11 February 1935 to Nea McCutcheon (1895-19?).*

story – the long story of a race enslaved and despised until it has to a great extent lost its pride in itself and come to court another by habit which is second nature'). Black rag dolls were also being made by hand before the golliwog.[198]

As in Britain, golliwogs were not only dolls and fancy-dress favourites but theatrical figures. Perhaps the largest public performance occurred in 1938 when up to 300 school boys danced as golliwogs in Geelong. At least one Australian cottage was called Golliwog; it was destroyed by fire in 1936. Like Britain, they were also lucky mascots: in the mid 1930s a golliwog travelled 7,000 miles in a caravan honeymoon trip. Nea Birtles said the doll 'proved of never-ending delight in natives with whom they came into contact'. Women in Australia and New Zealand made the dolls like their British counterparts. Mrs A. F. Boyce, known as the Golliwog Lady, created over 700 for charity while invalided at home in Remuera, New Zealand, in the late

1930s.[199]

In 1936 it was recalled that Australians serving in Egypt had mixed easily with their Caribbean counterparts whom they referred to as their 'colored cobbers' during the Great War. These 'chaps were black as your boot – big, strapping fellows, well-educated and musical' who were called golliwogs. It was suggested 'they did not seem to mind'.[200]

The figure's popularity was shown in 1913 when the Golliwog Bachelor Club was formed near Adelaide at Henley Beach South. It derived its name from the members' habit of parading in golliwog costumes. There was also the Golliwogs Social Club and the Victorian Golliwog Club.[201]

The Antipodean popularity continued into the 1950s when an eight-year-old girl composed 'The Sad Golliwog':

'Said the bear to the Golly –
*I don't like your face,*
*It's dreadfully dirty,*
*And quite a disgrace.*
So off went the Golly
To borrow some soap
And a basin of water.
And said *Now I hope*
*I'll soon get my face clean*
*And wash off the black.*
So he rubbed and he rubbed,
But alas and alack,
His face is the same.
It's round, black and fat.
*Oh, never mind, Golly,*
*We love you like that.*'[202]

*65. Three Australian children in fancy dress at Kooloonong, 1930.*

*66. Shop window in Sydney, 1937, including golliwog dolls.*

Australians interpreted the golliwog differently from the British by applying it to Indigenous people in Australia and in the Pacific Islands. For instance, in 1923 'Mr and Mrs Golliwog', the winners of a fancy-dress competition, were described as appearing like an 'aboriginal couple'.[203] That year among the dolls in one store were 'golliwog n*ggers' and in 1928 a South Seas Islands visitor to Sydney was called 'a true golliwog'.[204] A Brisbane newspaper also associated golliwogs with the South Seas in 1930. In this children's story a young girl is disappointed by a gift:

'*Why, it's a Kanaka dolly*, she cried. *Just a black n*gger*. For it was a golliwog, quite the loveliest one you ever saw, if you like golliwogs. His red and white striped trousers were of silk instead of cotton and he had a black satin swallow-tail coat and his quaint, ugly face wore the most comical, droll expression. But of course, he was ugly. Golliwogs have to be ugly.'[205]

Kanakas were Pacific Islands' workers employed in various colonies including Queensland where they were mostly Melanesian. In *The Green Mummy*, a novel published in 1908, two characters discussed Cockatoo, a Kanaka who had 'been captured when young by Pacific black-birders' and brought to England.

'*I do not like that Golliwog*, breathed Mrs Jasher to her host, when Cockatoo was at the sideboard. *He gives me the creeps.*

*Imagination, my dear lady. Pure imagination. Why should we not have a picturesque animal to wait upon us?*

*He would wait picturesquely enough at a cannibal feast*, suggested Archie with a laugh.

*Don't* murmured Lucy with a shiver. *I shall not be able to eat my dinner if you talk so.*

*Odd that Hope should say what he has said*, observed Braddock confidently to the widow. *Cockatoo comes from a cannibal island and doubtless has seen the consumption of flesh. No, no, my dear lady, do not look so alarmed. I don't think he has eaten any, as he was taken to Queensland long before he could participate in such banquets. He is a very decent animal.*'

It appears to have been commonplace to call Papua New Guineans golliwogs. In 1923 an Australian travel writer observed:

'Every little White girl and boy has a real live golliwog to play with in Samarai and the golliwog also looks after them for every moment of the day. More attentive than civilised nursemaids were these savages with their pierced ears and noses, their

> wrinkled faces and their appearance of being the perfect cannibal, and a strange contrast they were as they fussed over their tiny charges whose skin showed so white against theirs'.

During the Second World War, when there were Australian concerns regarding the treatment of the Indigenous people of New Guinea, one commentator noted 'The habit of calling them fuzzy-wuzzies is apt to result in their being thought of as amiable golliwogs, not as people with lives of their own who stand in need of understanding and help'. Another thought this terminology could legitimately result in Papuans calling White Australians 'Baldy Waldies' or 'Skinny Winnies'.[206]

As in Britain, golliwogs have a polarised legacy in Australia and New Zealand with former children recalling name-calling ('I have schoolyard memories of being called a golliwog, sausage lips and a w*g') and there is a continuing debate as to their place in modern society. Unlike Britain, where individuals with African heritage were called golliwogs, in Australasia the targets were, and continue to be, Aboriginal people, including Maori, and those from the islands of the South Pacific.[207] Also unlike Britain, golliwog dolls continue to be manufactured in Australia.

The golliwog has an overseas history largely independent of that of Britain and one that has marked differences.

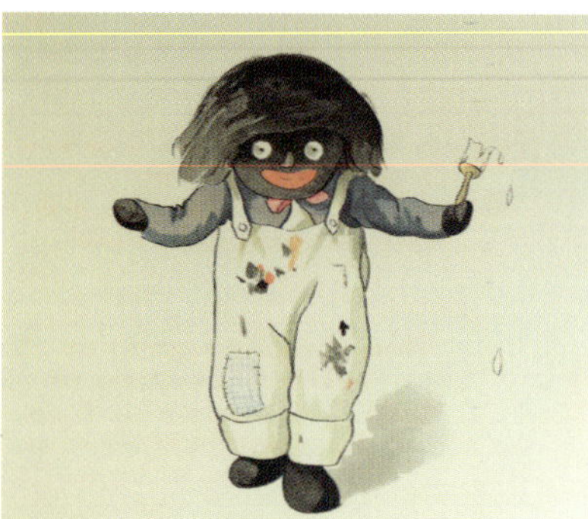

*67. By the late 1900s the public memory of Upton's golliwogg would be nearly forgotten.*

## CHAPTER 7

# Infatuation, the 1900s and 1910s

Society not only embraced the golliwogg during the first two decades of the twentieth century, it became a sensation.

In the early 1900s golliwogs became so embedded in the fabric of society that the word was extended in unusual ways even to describing women's early motoring clothing ('shapeless garments of shaggy fur, the sponge-bag caps, the double veils and protruding goggles which might appropriately have adorned an Arctic explorer's expedition') as 'golliwog'.[208] The character's success lay with the infatuation of children. This was apparently unknown to Florence Upton until she painted the portrait of a child who was holding a golliwogg:

> 'I have never seen a child in such a passion of love as she was for the time being with that Golliwogg, it was extraordinary. She had to keep on biting her lips to keep from smiling. Sometimes she pressed him to her with almost quivering passion, saying under her breath *Oh, you darling*. It was a revelation to me.'[209]

Golliwoggs captured the hearts of children not only in books but in public shows and charity fund-raising. They also consumed adults who used them as good luck charms.

The figure featured in pantomimes as early as 1898 and in plays such as *The Golliwog* in 1910 as well as in musical revues.[210] Stan Laurel (1890-1965), of Laurel and Hardy, and Arthur Askey (1900-1982) were perhaps the two best-known actors to portray

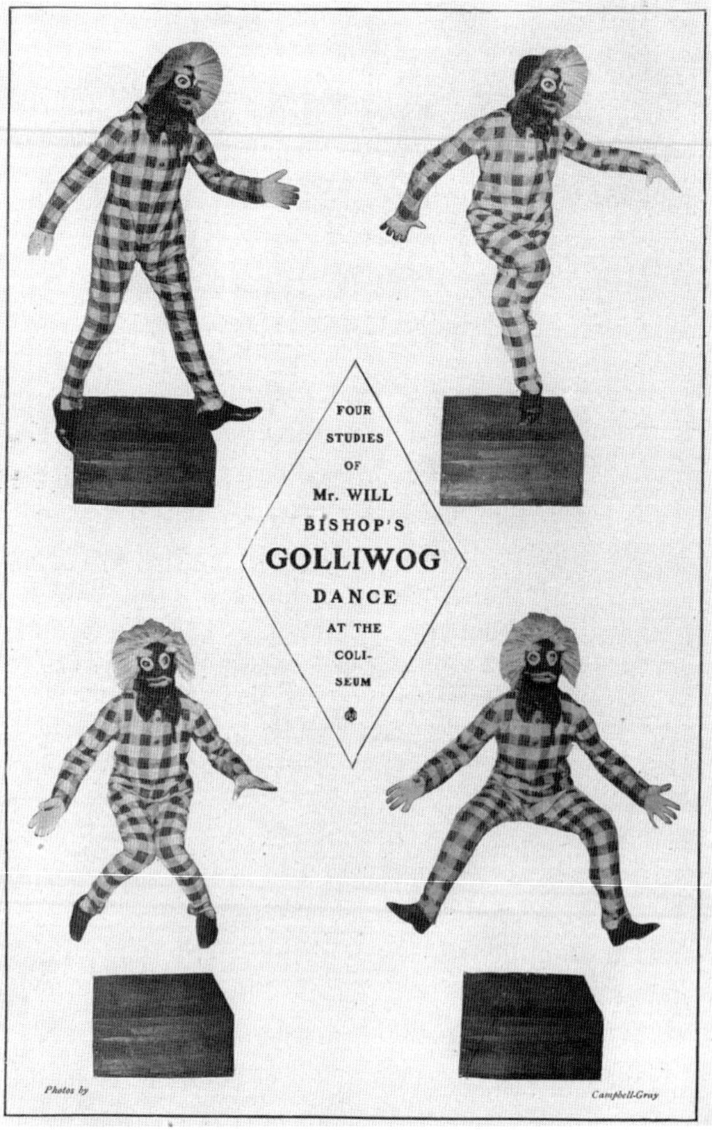


*68. Will Bishop's Golliwog Dance remained popular from 1896 through into the twentieth century.*

golliwogs.[211] It was claimed, presumably because he had used blackface, that Fred Astaire (1899-1987) had been known as the 'Nebraska Golliwog' when he worked in vaudeville in the early 1900s.[212] In 1905 a 'musical extravaganza', entitled *My Golliwog* ran at the Colosseum in London, involved a clockwork dance. Films included *The Old Favourite and the Ugly Golliwog* in 1908 followed by *The Ragtime Golliwog Man* in 1913. *Golliwog's Motor Accident* was released in 1912 under that title in America but was originally *In Golliwog Land*, a British film. It was the first colour animation film and mixed live action with puppetry. It depicted 'the antics of golliwogs in a motor accident, how they deal with apples and apple pies and making a bouquet'.[213] One of the more unusual entertainments took place in 1909: 'The Living Golliwog' appeared at the American Roller Skating Palace in London. He was 'the funniest thing on skates'. Meanwhile, Reading's Roller Skating Rink had 'The Golliwog', 'the champion skating comedian of the world'.[214] Another London attraction the following year was the Golliwog Wiggle Woggle, an early type of bumper car.[215]

'Living Golliwogs' were part of a wider element of the golliwog world: not only did they make theatrical appearances but men and women dressed as golliwogs for street processions and parades. They were often part of fetes and fairs including events such as Bonfire Night.

Actresses kept golliwoggs for good luck: Irene Vanbrugh (1872-1949), of Heavitree near Exeter, owned a small one as a mascot and attached to it were other charms.[216] They became prevalent in dressing rooms. Marjorie Hume (1900-1976), the film actress, kept them 'both big and small, of high and low estate, smile, frown or glare at you from perilous perches on the walls, from the safer seats of shelves and tables or from the

*69. Birthday cards featuring golliwogs, early 1900s.*

brilliantly-illuminated throne of their owner's dressing glass'.[217] Cecilia Gold was another who in 1908 reportedly had many hundreds of small golliwogs and would not perform unless wearing one. Another actress decorated her dressing room with the golliwogs thrown onto the stage during her 'Golliwog Doll Dance' in 'Aladdin' in 1906. 'Quaint way of showing their appreciation, wasn't it?' said Carrie Moore (1882-1956).[218] Evie Greene (1875-1917), also a stage actress, was noted for her golliwog collection.[219] This theatrical custom was observed by a novelist in 1909 who described a dressing room:

> 'And, over all, she hung her gollywog, a hairy doll, white-collared, red-waistcoated, with, in its black face, under the bristling hair, two shining tacks by way of eyes. It was the protecting idol. Not that Lily, ever faithful to the Church of England, believed much in golliwogs; but, like most music-hall people, she felt safer when she knew it was there'.[220]

Jose Collins (1887-1958) collected more than 70 golliwogs; her favourite was her mascot, Sambo.[221]

When in 1914 W. H. Berry (1870-1951), a British comic actor, was asked about his golliwog mascot he explained 'It was thrown to me on the stage of the last night of *The Merry Widow* and it bears the inscription *With love from the boys and girls of the gallery on the O.P. side.* It has never left my dressing-room since.'[222] Likewise, in 1919 an Australian comedienne said 'I wouldn't be without that golliwog for the world even if he has lost nearly all his hair. He's lucky. And I have had him so long.' Attached to his red trousers was a card bearing the inscription *Kia Ora*, New Zealandic for Good Luck.[223]

Specially-composed music included a polka and Claude Debussy's (1862-1918) 'Golliwog's Cake Walk'. In 1918 Ivor Novello (1893-1951) wrote the music for 'Goblin Golliwog

Trees'.[224] In a curious example of reverse cultural transference, in 1913 American minstrels from Mississippi sang the recently-released 'Rag-time golliwog man' at a performance in Tottenham.[225]

Blackface was essential in live portrayals of golliwogs, and by extension, of Black men and women. In 1906 a London variety performance featured a golliwog who sang in the tradition of minstrels but without the repertoire of 'plantation songs':

> 'Florence Yaymen is quaint, original and resourceful, three essentials of success in the variety theatre. Costumed and made up as a knock-kneed female golliwog, she, in true n*gger style, asks her audience to *Come and take this little picaninny home*. Her facial expression and inimitable laugh send the audience into fits of uncontrollable laughter'.

It was not until 1963 that the first talking golliwog doll was created. He had a Jamaican accent and said 'I's a-watching you'.[226]

Golliwogs featured in grassroots charity fundraising. Private individuals, mostly children and women, made an extraordinary number to sell for good causes. Competitions were held to guess the name of a golliwog such as Aubrey, Fri, George, Horatio, Israel, Jeremy, Moses, Nebo, Sambo and Timothy. Male and female performers, many of whom were amateurs and some children, organised themselves as the Golliwog Band, Golliwog Club, Golliwog Dancers, Golliwog Dramatic Club, Golliwog Dramatic Society, Golliwog Minstrel Troupe, Golliwog Minstrels, Golliwog Pierrot Troupe, Golliwog Trio, Golliwog Troupe, the Original Golliwogs and the Three Golliwog Girls.[227] It was claimed in 1916 that the popularity of golliwog dances in revues encouraged 'fluffy-haired girls' to lop their locks 'to give themselves an up-to-date effect'.[228] The Great War saw the formation of Golliwog Funds and Societies including one at Dursley in Gloucestershire; these philanthropic groups helped

70. *German country dance music entitled 'Mr Gollywog Schottische' by Henri Dupret, c1908.*

71. *'The Gollywog Two-Step', 1909.*

72. *'Goblin Golliwog Trees' from Tabs, 1918.*

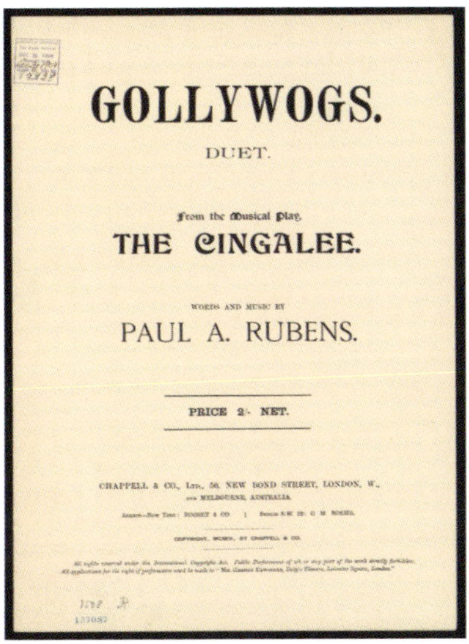


73. *'Gollywogs', duet, 1904 from The Cingalee.*

wounded servicemen.[229] Golliwogs featured in adults' social clubs such as the Brunswick Villagers Golliwog Club in Islington (1909) and Ye Olde Ancient Order of Golliwogs at Gravesend (1910) as well as sports clubs including the Treherbert Golliwog Club which promoted hockey and cricket (1922).[230]

*74. The Manor Park and District Golliwog Society was formed by a group of friends during the Great War to help wounded servicemen.*

A charity event in 1915 elicited widespread uncertainty about the choice of golliwogs:

> 'One question everybody who bought a golliwog was asking yesterday was *Why a golliwog*? Nobody actually knew.
>
> He was of all colours and of all sizes from the little black or red or brown figure that the workers pinned in every purchaser's buttonhole up to the super golliwog that figured prominently in the procession and was fitted with an ingenious mechanism inside him, and had electric globes for eyes.
>
> But once a golliwog always a golliwog. He never varied in shape. The question was, why he figured as a patriotic emblem? The only possible explanation that one of the workers could offer in reply to the question was that it was because of his *frightfulness* and in view of the fact that he was eventually *sold*.'[231]

Upton's book sales were waning in 1909, when the last of her works was published, and the death of her mother Bertha three years later made it more difficult to recommence the series. The following year the *Golliwog News* appeared; this newspaper reported the events happening in Golliwogland but it was the work of another writer, the editor of the *Broadstairs Echo*.[232] Other writers had by then taken up the golliwog.

Dolls remained popular and a key factor in their prevalence was that they could be made cheaply at home: rag dolls were composed of cloth oddments. Newspapers regularly printed instructions. It is likely that the majority of golliwogs were made by many tens of thousands of women across the country and Empire. Miss Gracie Howell was one of them. A golliwog had been her only childhood toy while resident at the Sisters of Nazareth Orphanage in Australia and as an adult in 1953 she knitted dozens for the institution when it moved to Belfast in Ireland.[233]

They were also made by the poor. In the months leading up to Christmas in 1910 three men, six women and three girls from two families who lived in a four-roomed house in the East End of London produced golliwogs for street hawkers. They were sold for a penny:

> 'Their faces and bodies are made of painted clay, their arms and legs of hair springs, with little clay balls for hands and feet, and their bodies are wrapped in black fur.'[234]

Golliwogs were worn by women in charm bracelets[235] and men kept them as personal mascots for competitive sports. For many years the official mascot for Birmingham City was a golliwog. In 1909 a 'comic' football match took place outside Exeter at Topsham with local men playing a team of golliwogs. Similar teams played polo at Weston-Super-Mare and hockey at Derby. It was the mascot for a balloonist in a cross-Channel race in 1913. The golliwog was adopted by celebrities such as

Send them
victorious
Happy and
glorious

Oh isn't it
Toby they'll
be home
again

Everybody
in some way
WHAT
WILL
YOU DO?
DO IT NOW!
I've brought you
some recruits!

Golly is a Tommy brave and Teddy a jolly Jack ...
One dolly is a V.A.D. the other is a W.A.A.C. ...
I'm very proud of them because you really must admit
They're trying just their very best to do their little bit.

Sir Ernest Shackleton (1874-1922) who in 1914 placed one in the *Aurora* and another in the *Endurance* for his exploration of Antarctica.[236] The Young Zulu King, otherwise known as Giuseppe Di Melfi (1897-1971), a professional boxer, was known for carrying a 'Zulu Golliwog' into his matches.[237] Aviator Keith Macpherson Smith (1890-1955) famously wired his pink and black golliwog Percy to his helmet on his flight from England to Australia in 1919.[238]

The craze for golliwogs as mascots had begun in 1908. Consuelo Montagu (1853-1909), Duchess of Manchester, the Cuban-American heiress, was reportedly given one by Edward VII at Biarritz. It was claimed she constantly kept it with her, particularly when she played bridge.[239] Following the outbreak of the Great War, the golliwog found fresh favour as amulets. They bore little resemblance to minstrels, some were even made from acorns. At this time an epidemic of 'gollywogitis' was reported in the military hospitals at Leeds where wounded servicemen made thousands to sell for charity. That same year another writer described their popularity in a Surrey hospital as 'golliwog fever':

> 'It was introduced by a new patient who arrived with a curious little bundle of coloured wool in his buttonhole, which he spoke of affectionately as his golliwog. The following week more of these quaint mascots appeared with a new convoy, and one wearer carried a small cardboard box and little pieces of coloured fluff were noticed clinging to his coat. In five minutes he was busy, wool all round him, skilfully wielding a large pair of scissors with an interested but rather pitying audience about him. The next day the germ had many victims. It affected them in two ways with a creative fever or a collective fever, the latter being most common in female sufferers.'

*75. Opposite page: Four patriotic postcards featuring Golliwogs, 1914-1919.*

The outbreak turned into an epidemic:

'The first golliwog was a simple creature, not more than two inches long and only of two colours. But a victim of the creative germ, having an original and artistic mind, suggested a three-coloured golliwog, and before long rainbow-hued specimens glared at us from 29 buttonholes. Another found that diminutive gollies (this abbreviation was adopted three days after the outbreak) appealed to the feminine victims of the collective germ, so microscopic specimens became the rage. A short-sighted collector demanded something he could see, and a creative genius who longed to outdo the popularity of the microscopic inventor, introduced the mammoth.'

The enthusiasm continued:

'Golliwogs were produced by the score; golliwogs fat, golliwogs lean (according to wool supplies); in sober colours and gay, every possible combination and contrast of colours was tried. Nurses appeared wearing the mascots in their caps and tucked in their belts and pinned in front of their bicycles. The climax was reached when the Medical Officer was seen with a golliwog five inches long and three inches round the waist, and with an oriental colour scheme, in his coat. We said firmly *This thing must cease*. Strong measures were taken, wool supplies were cut off, scissors confiscated, and any patient seen eyeing a quiet corner and having a soft parcel about his person received immediate orders to take a walk. But the germ had so strong a hold that these precautions were not sufficient to stamp it out. Darns were carefully unpicked, knives were purloined, and grey, greasy golliwogs appeared, made in the dead of night by the light of a match. The disease was not finally stamped out until every patient was discharged, and all members of the staff given a holiday.'[240]

As discussed earlier, it was probably during these years that the word golliwog became a pejorative term for Black men,

*76. An early twentieth-century golliwog postcard with a cricket theme.*

women and children. In 1907 the Aldershot Military Tournament featured units from across the empire including policemen from Fiji who were dubbed 'the golliwogs' because of their appearance; they were 'bare-legged, with white linen kilts, blue coats with broad red belts and black faces, their striking appearance was completed by shocks of matted, orange-coloured hair, a colour the natives pride themselves on and which is obtained by treating the hair with lime.'[241]

The golliwogg leapt from the pages of children's books into British theatres and cinemas. At the same time it became a staple of local fundraising partly through perhaps its strangest incarnation, that of the lucky amulet.

CHAPTER 8

# Permeating society, the 1920s to the 1940s

From the 1920s to the 1940s the golliwog continued to be a well-known facet of everyday life in Britain.

When Florence Upton died in 1922 a golliwog was placed amongst the bouquets of her funeral flowers. The figure's popularity survived her death.[242] While new golliwog products were manufactured including such items as children's slippers,[243] dolls remained the most popular incarnation. Most were owned by children but they even decorated car bonnets including that of Richard Acland (1906-1990) of Killerton near Exeter. During the parliamentary election of 1929 his car bore a woollen golliwog in the Liberal Party colours.[244] In 1924 a poem, 'Mascots', appeared in the press:

> 'Say can this world, with all its follies,
> Boast of a greater 'neath the stars
> Than mascots, golliwogs or dollies
> Which decorate our motor cars?
>
> A woollen golliwog or kitten,
> Is borne to shield from pending fate;
> Are those who bear it never smitten?
> If so, our papers fail to state.
>
> This fetish of the heathen n*gger,
> Which from the land of *Ju-Ju* sprang,

So rude, uncouth in face and figure,
Its praise no decent n*gger sang.
Yet English folks of every station
With some weird mascot deck their cars;
As well might take upon probation
Small images of Jove or Mars.

Do those replete with superstition
Place no reliance on the power
Of Heaven, and there to make petition
To keep them safe in danger's hour?

To guard from ill, if the objective,
The golliwog you can't extol;
A silent prayer is more effective
Than any ugly woollen doll.

All superstition faith abuses,
And all its evils none can tell,
But vain must be the faith that chooses
Both Heaven and golliwog as well.'[245]

By 1925 Bristol Bili was the mascot of students at the University of Bristol and greeted the king and queen when they visited; their golliwog mascot was positioned over the university gates.[246] In Paris in about 1927 it became fashionable to hang dolls, including golliwogs, inside cars' rear windows. The fad spread as far as Australia.[247]

Golliwogs were popular in fancy-dress competitions and dances. In 1923 Cecil Parlby's costume was singled out for praise at a charity ball held by the Children's League in Plymouth; it was reported that his 'smiling black face with a perfect mop of black wool covering his head made a thorough good golliwog'.[248]

*77. Opposite page: Upton's depictions of the golliwogg's adventures.*

GOLLIWOGG'S
CIRCUS

THE CRASSIE

PEACE

Robertson's popularity gave rise in late 1920s to a new fancy dress character, the Golden Shred Golliwog.[249]

In these decades foreign races were commonly depicted in fancy dress. At Clovelly Court near Bideford in 1929, for instance, Master J. Bromell won a prize for his golliwog costume while another boy was an 'Indian'. Meanwhile, at Exeter in 1926 not only was there a golliwog but an Arab and Gunner Cooper won a prize as a female impersonator for his Eastern Lady. Other common costumes, some reflecting British colonies, were of 'Red Indians' or 'Indian Chiefs', 'Chinese Coolies', 'Snake Charmers' and Zulu warriors.[250] In 1920 a procession of those in fancy dress at a ball in Ramsgate was described:

> 'Eastern brides were represented in force; the diaphanous attire of a harem girl made her a conspicuous figure; Cleopatra was represented by two ladies in contrasting costumes; Japanese and Chinese maids were sandwiched between a living golliwog and a lady representing [W. G.] Nixev's black lead; Monsieur Beaucaire found himself near a convict. A Parisian Apache and a full-blooded Indian found a place in the parade with a Chinese mandarin.'[251]

*78. German postcard of five girls with their golliwogs, undated.*

The Fancy Dress Subscription Ball at the East Africa Turf Club at Mombassa in 1910 attracted not only a golliwog but an Egyptian, Spanish gipsy, South American brigand, Pathan peasant, Irish girl, Indian, 'Chinaman', Italian peasant, Boulogne fishwife, native labourer, Negro minstrel, Albanian, Arabian lady, Dutch girl, Irish colleen and a Spanish girl.[252]

Numerous social occasions featuring golliwogs took place such as when in 1923, at Yealmpton near Plymouth, twelve Brownies, the juniors in the Girl Guides, performed 'A Christmas Dream' as golliwogs; the children were noted as 'the life of the play'.[253] They were also a popular figure for children's parties including in 1926 when a golliwog assisted Santa Claus in distributing presents in Exmouth. They were appropriated for adult events: when a golliwog dance took place at Mafeking, South Africa, in 1923 each dancer was decorated with a woollen golliwog and had to find a partner wearing one of the same colour.[254] In 1927 it was claimed that golliwog heads were worn by women in London in their garters as a fashion item.[255]

Fundraisers entitled 'Golliwog Days' took place across England. In 1922 one was held in Tiverton for the Boy Scouts; 1,000 golliwogs

*79. An advertisement for Golliwog Day held for Kensington & Fulham General Hospital, 29 October 1918.*

were sold. Two years later another took place in South Molton for the North Devon Infirmary. In the 1903s some one hundred pounds, the equivalent in modern money of five thousand pounds, was raised on Golliwog Day in Lincoln; it purchased shoes for poor children.[256] There were also Golliwog Flag Days, such as took place in Birmingham in 1920, in which paper golliwogs were sold.[257] A young Manchester woman made 40,000 golliwogs to raise money for a local hospital: each one took her six minutes to make.[258] Dolls continued to be sold commercially including even on the *Carinthia*, a passenger liner which crossed the Atlantic.[259] Other fundraisers included the Golliwog Club's third annual variety and dramatic performance in Croydon in aid of the St Giles' Home for British Lepers.[260]

New music featuring golliwogs included 'Giggling Golliwog', a slow fox trot, by the Stellar Dance Band in 1929 and 'Golliwog on the Loose' by Len Stevens (1910-1989) in 1947.[261] One of the new jazz dances in 1921, along with the alligator azzle and the brontosaurus bump, was the golliwog glide.[262] There were innumerable golliwog-themed dances including the 'latest Gollywog Brazilian caterpillar crawl' captured by John Galsworthy (1867-1933), the novelist and playwright in 1915 ('For, sidelong, with a mouth widened till it nearly reached her ears, her legs straddling and her stomach writing, she was moving incomparably across the stage. Her face, twisted on her neck, at an alarming angle, was distorted to a strange, inimitable hideousness').[263]

In 1922 the golliwog entered national politics when Prime Minister Bonar Law was called a 'wriggling golliwog'. Three years later Liberal Prime Minister David Lloyd George (1863-1945) said the Labour Government was 'sitting timid, like scared golliwogs, not knowing what to do'. A political observer

*80. The Warwickshire stained-glass window with the golliwog doll, 1933.*

suggested that the phrase was 'amusing enough' but unlikely to stick.[264] The novelty of the golliwog gave rise to it being used to describe society. Various writers from 1918 to 1928 called this 'The Golliwog Age' either because of its effect on morals, art or women's clothing.[265]

Public enthusiasm continued in the 1930s in similar ways but there were variations and additions. For instance, schools held races in which children ran dressed as golliwogs; an Ilfracombe school in 1930 was one of many to hold such races.[266] In 1933 a stained-glass window was installed in Kingsbury parish church in Warwickshire: it depicted Christ with several children, one of whom held a golliwog in her hand.[267]

In 1937 and 1938 the 'Golliwog Man' targeted women on an estate in Hornchurch in Essex. He was given that nickname because his hair stood on end.[268]

The Second World War bolstered the character's role as a fundraiser; it was sold at such events in Devon as the Plymouth Spitfire Fund, Mrs Churchill's Red Cross Aid for Russia Fund at Shaldon and the Prisoners of War Fund in Exeter.[269] A new company was registered in 1946: Golliwog Ices Ltd was based in London.[270] At the end of the decade, on 14 December 1949, the Bishop of Exeter launched a toy drive for children in hospitals and orphanages: he fastened a symbolic golliwog to a Christmas tree at the Gaumont Theatre in Exeter.[271]

Race was only obliquely referred to or ignored such as in 1931 when Vera Brittain (1893-1970), the writer interested in socialism and pacifism, overlooked race in her commending golliwogs to parents as an indispensable inhabitant of nurseries. By then they had become temporarily unavailable in shops but she eventually managed to replace the family's worn-out golliwog. Brittain felt its meaningless was the most important attribute. She wrote his 'grotesque indefiniteness may be, and is, synonymous with anything his owner wants him to represent'. Her son regarded the golliwog as 'a species of tribal deity, an anthropomorphic potentate', a projection of self and his junior.[272] Likewise, in 1925 a former child reminisced about her golliwog: 'Above all there was the Dutch dolls' hero and mine, with his coal-black, silky mane, soot-black face (certainly I never misliked him for his complexion), his linen-button eyes, commanding nose, engaging mouth, blue coat, red breeches and all!'[273]

The golliwog maintained his appeal among British children and adults during the 1920s, 1930s and 1940s and was accepted without question.

*81. Rocking card by Raphael Tuck, early 1900s, which had fallen out of fashion by the late 1900s. It was entitled 'The glad golliwog' with the verses 'To jump this merry child upon my knee,' said golliwog, 'is just the fun for me! she used to seem afraid because my hair is black as coals, but now she doesn't care; whatever toys her aunts and uncles send, she chooses me to be her favorite friend!'*

CHAPTER 9

# Falling out of favour, the 1950s and 1960s

There were implications for the golliwog from the fall of the British Empire and immigration from the Caribbean and the Indian subcontinent.

## 1950s

The golliwog remained as prevalent following the Second World War as it had been in the decades beforehand. For instance, it was the chosen motif for the illuminated lamps at Southsea during its Festival of Britain events and a young German actor standing five feet four inches high played a living golliwog on stage at Blackpool's Tower Circus. Sales of the doll were still high and golliwogs were even called by one commentator, along with teddy bears, the 'old-timers of the nursery', that is the favourites toys who were 'ageless heart-throbs' who had seen off competition from Humpty Dumpty, Felix the Cat, Bonzo, Dismal Desmond, Mickey Mouse and Muffin the Mule. Thousands of badges continued to be sent from Robertson's and not only did Enid Blyton write new books but they were supplemented by Garnie Ritchie's *The Golliwog* (1950), Ruth Ainsworth's *Rufty Tufty the Golliwog* (1952), Jenny Taylor's *Ann's Golliwog* (1953), Wolf Mankowitz's *Majollika and Company* (1955), *The Gollywog Picture Book* (New York, 1955), *The So Long Book of Gollywog Tales* (1955), Mollie Clarke's *The Bad Golliwog* (1956), Clifford Webb's

*Magic Island* (1956) and C. Fraser-Simpson's *The Adventures of Golly Smith* (1956) among others. The publisher of Rufty Tufty suggested 'he's a lazy golliwog, an untidy golliwog, a curious, interfering golliwog but you can't help liking him all the same' while a reviewer commented that 'the golliwogs turn out to be nice middle-class English boys and girls'. In *Rufty Tufty Makes a House* two children met their golliwog's family on a tropical island. Innumerable other authors featured golliwogs in short stories. New music included 'Jumping Golliwog' by Max Marten in 1959.[274]

Golliwogs remained highly visible. A seventeen-foot moving golliwog was erected by a Manchester store for its Christmas display in 1958. It may have been the biggest golliwog yet

*82. A golliwog marionette, produced in England for the German market, on which is written on the back 'I've just looked in to say good day and please, I hope you'll let me stay, although as you will quickly see, I've brought my baby wogs with me', undated.*

known although there was also a 'giant' golliwog advertisement in Piccadilly Square.[275] They also appeared in unexpected ways. In 1955 a lucky golliwog featured in the trial of a soldier accused of murdering his wife's first husband. German-born Mrs Mia Emmett-Dunne (c1926-?), described by the press as 'lovely' and a 'pretty' former nightclub singer, was travelling on a German autobahn to collect a golliwog she had left behind when her car overturned during a cloudburst. She explained 'I just *had* to get the doll. I must not be parted from it.'[276]

The word golliwog was embraced in new ways. In 1954 Johannes Adelbert Hopmann, a German agricultural labourer, renamed his Berkshire home 'The Golliwogs'.[277] The Golliwog Toy Shop opened in Belfast in 1954 and continued until its lease expired in 1970. Likewise, Mr Golliwog opened in Esher in 1959 and remained in business until the early 1970s. New designs for children's clothing in 1955 included fabric with 'black golliwogs with red pants and yellow jumpers on a white background'. It was at this time that a London firm manufactured upper-end children's dresses with the Golliwog brand name.[278]

With a lack of racial sensitivity, that is to a modern sensibility as astonishing as it is shocking, in 1955 a newspaper journalist advised how to transform a child into a golliwog:

> 'This is contrived from no more than a mop of thick, black wool surmounting a well-blackened face and neck. Large white circles painted on around the eyes and a bright scarlet mouth make this one very realistic.'[279]

Likewise, a year earlier another columnist outlined the rules of a new children's game, 'No Black, No White', in which neither word could be used. Suggested questions included:

> '*If you scrubbed a golliwog's face, what colour would it be?*

One feels tempted to answer, *Still black of course.*'[280]

There were signs of an awareness of race as the first great immigration from the Caribbean took place and the empire disintegrated. In 1957 Chelsea Town Hall hosted the Centre for Spastic Children's Golliwog Ball. It may have been because of racial sensitivities that its chairman said 'the name golliwog doesn't have any special significance. We had to call the ball *something*.'[281] The previous year, when parts of Britain were adjusting to becoming more multi-cultural, a children's story appeared in a Birmingham newspaper and captured the novelty. Inky, a London schoolboy who had recently emigrated from Jamaica, met 'little blonde Minna Grey' who was astonished to see his likeness to her golliwog. With a happy smile she said 'Oh, you're Black like him! You can be his daddy!'[282]

The *Black and White Minstrel Show* began in 1958 as did *Nutshell*, a programme for Associated-Rediffusion. It featured Friday, a golliwog made in Johannesburg for Redvers Kyle (1929-2015), the show's presenter.[283] The colours of golliwogs were also explored. In 1956 'The White Golliwog', a projected television programme, depicted Britain as a tropical island in which 'the native population of Britain will be Black instead of White. The story will show what happens when White people immigrate in increasing numbers.'[284] This was also when Chalky, the white-faced golliwog, first appeared on British television: he was a friend of Twizzle, another puppet.[285] Several decades earlier, in the early 1930s, a London girl had been short of cloth remnants and utilised white linen in order to make a Black golliwog with oculocutaneous albinism; her white golliwog had red hair and she called him Albi, her abbreviation for Albino. But, in pre-Caribbean immigration Britain, adults subsequently ridiculed her golliwog for not being Black.[286] Other golliwogs, however, had red hair including the female golliwogs sold at Boots in 1928: they wore velvet dresses and had red curls, earrings and 'slave bangles of white bone'.[287]

In 1958 a sixteen-year-old girl complained to her local Coventry newspaper of the treatment given to a Nigerian girl who was head prefect; they called her a golliwog. Pat Beamish asked 'Is this justifiable? Should an innocent girl be forced to suffer because of the colour of her skin? Those of us who knew her well were horrified to find some of our own number so prejudiced. What can we expect from others less favoured?'[288] In 1958 a Derbyshire vicar argued that golliwogs had a detrimental effect on children because they fostered racial mistrust and nurtured a colour bar.[289]

**1960s**

It was in 1965 that a British toy-maker attempted to diversify its product range and break into the American toy market by producing a white-faced golliwog.[290] Meanwhile, in Britain golliwog toys were advertised as ideal gifts and fancy-dress competitions often included golliwogs. They featured in various cultural discourses including as a device to explore dark issues such as on 6 June 1962 when, at a theatre in Dunedin, *Conversations with a Golliwog* was performed on stage. This play, written by New Zealander Alexander Guyan (1933-1991), explored the mental health of a fourteen-year-old girl through Boswell, her five-foot golliwog.[291] The following year a feature-length film, with the working title *Golliwog*, which was renamed *Tomorrow at Ten*, told the story of a kidnapped boy who had a bomb sewn into his golliwog. The background to the abduction centres on the kidnapper's troubled childhood memories of his golliwog and his parents' nightclub, The Golliwog Club.[292]

In 1964 Cilla Black, then called the 'golden girl of show

*83. Gyll Webber in Conversation with a Golliwog at the Elmwood Theatre, Christchurch, New Zealand, 1964.*

business', was given a giant golliwog on her twenty-first birthday. Also that year a Sunday School banner at Alsager near Crewe was made which depicted 'Christ, with a coloured child in his arms, with a fair-haired child offering a golliwog to the coloured child.'[293] In 1965 a dozen prisoners in a Shrewsbury gaol sewed a thousand golliwog dolls a month[294] and in 1967 the Golliwog Boutique opened in Walsall: golliwogs featured in the window, a local band renamed The Golliwogs played to customers and the staff wore red, blue and white-striped costumes.[295] Another set of musicians, The Golliwog, described as 'a real with-it group', appeared at Penrhyn Bay in 1969.[296] This band appears to have been different from Creedence Clearwater Revival which had been called Golliwog until 1968: American bandmembers had been pressured by their management to follow the British groups then dominating American music and it was suggested the new name conveyed Britain ('the British soldiers got to calling these dolls w*gs, like a golliwog. And sometimes they even called the people golliwogs or w*gs. So this little voodoo doll is a very important thing in British history. See, we want you guys to seem like you're British – part of the hip, British musical invasion!'). Golliwog was also the name of a new women's hat, described as zany and crazy, made of Mongolian wool.[297] By 1967 the Golliwog Café, in Penarth near Cardiff, had opened.[298]

However, the decade was marked by increasing social tensions. In 1960 a woman from Bury St Edmunds wrote to her local newspaper:

> 'May I make a very strong protest about the so-called decorations which have been fixed to the outside walls of the Corn Exchange especially the hideous *golliwogs*. I have enjoyed the real friendship of many persons from our wider Commonwealth areas and know the very deep hurt inflicted on their minds by such images.

A *golliwog* is taken by a man of dark skin to be a personally insulting reminder of the scorn once exhibited to slaves.

This may seem absurd to us, but I can assure you that it causes very real offence in large numbers of cases, even lasting bitterness to sensitive minds. Has Christmas nothing of beauty or friendship for us to show forth to our maybe lonely and introspective visitors who are far from their own homes?'[299]

In 1965 the director of the Institute of Race Relations thought the figures caused harm because 'children identify coloured people with golliwogs and this helps to build up a picture of the Negro as an inferior being'. Toy sales fell in 1966: 'that innocent, one-time favourite, the golliwog, no longer sells as well as it used to do'. An established manufacturer attributed this to Britain's growing racial awareness which had followed recent immigration. Only three golliwogs were at the Christmas show of the British Toy Manufacturers and one representative admitted exports were insignificant: 'We've never really been able to sell them in Africa or Malaysia and they never caught on in Europe'. He added that golliwogs were unknown in America. British sales were strongest in expensive retail outlets such as Harrods and Fortnum & Mason. They were made by Basingstoke firm Cooncraft whose spokesman explained 'the name just sort of came to us'.[300]

In 1964 a fourteen-year-old boy of African heritage was kicked unconscious on his second day at school in Ealing. He had been called a golliwog by his attacker.[301] In 1967 more than two hundred Black immigrants signed a petition calling on the BBC to terminate the Black and White Minstrel Show. A representative said 'the objection to the show is that it caricatures coloured people as unintelligent, idiot coons or golliwogs'. The following year the National Committee for Commonwealth Immigrants published *Psychology of Racial Prejudice*. Its author warned that golliwogs were anti-social characters who made children fearful of Black people.[302] That year an indignant Leicester resident despaired of a proposed ban of golliwog dolls and questioned whether minstrel shows and the Robertson golly would survive. Some of those fears were about to become reality.[303]

In the last year of the decade one journalist reported that the British public was fascinated by the appearance of twenty-one-year-old Marsha Hunt (1946-) in *Hair* because she looked like a 'delicious golliwog'. Hunt was known for her Afro haircut.[304]

Despite continuing public enthusiasm, it was during the post-war years that meaningful objections began to be made about golliwogs: large-scale immigration from the colonies brought the British face-to-face with those people being denigrated by the golliwog.

*84. Female and possibly male musicians dressed as golliwogs in an Armistice Day procession at Brisbane, Australia. Each individual has a black cloth face covering, carries an American flag and one holds a golliwog doll. Such events were common in the early 1900s but were increasingly viewed as inappropriate in the second half of the century.*

## CHAPTER 10

# The golliwog's demise, 1970 to 2001

In the late twentieth century the golliwog became a figure of the past with an uncertain future in society.

In addition to a proposed ban in Britain on the grounds of children's mental health, two foreign governments had banned the golliwogs for reasons connected with race. In the 1930s the Nazis outlawed sales of black-faced dolls in the interests of racial purity; they were 'non-Aryan'. One German newspaper asked its readers 'Must we have n*gger dolls'? In 1940 a circular of the Ministry of the Interior specified that it was forbidden to sell, purchase, distribute or repair golliwogs or any dolls of a non-Aryan nature. Satirical lines entitled 'Golliwog in Exile' were published in *Punch*:

> 'A golliwog and German-made, I stand,
> Sinless and exiled, innocent but banned,
> Over the frontier of my native land.
>
> They came upon me when the night was deep;
> In the calm night they came when ill things creep,
> And decent persons give the hours to sleep.'[305]

Nearly a generation later, in 1959, the South African government banned *Toyland*, a children's story book, because in it a White girl kissed a golliwog: '*Look at his little black face*, said Amanda. *Isn't he sweet*? And she gives him a hug and a kiss.'[306]

*85. A post-war German golly from Little Dolly and Her Friend Golly, 1960.*

## 1970s and 1980s

In the early years of the 1970s there were signs of continuing interest in, if not support for, golliwogs. In 1970 a Wolverhampton woman wrote to her local newspaper to explain that when her daughter was born two boys in her neighbourhood gave her their favourite toys, a teddy and a golliwog. Mrs Edna Sadler, who herself as a child had been ridiculed by being called a golliwog, wrote they 'are my coloured daughter's bedtime favourites because love came with them.' In the early 1970s the

Ulster Defence Association broadcast as Radio Golliwog, a pirate radio station. In 1971 an eighteen-year-old author published her first children's book *The White Golliwog*[307] and British golliwog exporters reportedly had a 'tremendous' reception from American buyers including from two large West Coast stores.[308] That year the Black and White Minstrels held a charity sale which included a six-feet-tall golliwog which bore all the signatures of current and former minstrels.[309] In 1973 a Glaswegian bride's *Avante garde* outfit was notable. She and her husband wore identical white slacks and cape jackets but it was her replacement of a bouquet with a golliwog that attracted more attention.[310] That year Scottish funk band Average White Band released their album *Show Your Hand* with a white golliwog on the cover. In 1974 an abandoned baby chimp at Dudley Zoo was given a golliwog for a companion[311] and that year Agnetha Fältskog, of ABBA, recorded a music single entitled 'Golliwog'.

*86. The HMS Crichton golliwog.*

In 1982 a cocktail created for under-eighteen-year-olds at the Hare & Hounds in Kingskerswell in Devon was named the Golliwog and fancy-dress costumes of golliwogs continued such as those worn by twenty-four brownies and guides for the annual carnival procession in Chudleigh.[312] In 1983 HMS *Crichton* adopted the golly as its mascot and Robertson's presented a special badge to each crew member of the minesweeper. As late as 1990 a Cornish firm was awarded a substantial contract to supply a store in Nigeria with golliwogs.[313] The following year Mike McKenzie, noted by a football journalist as 'Britain's most successful Black manager', revealed 'I've got a little black golliwog which I always carry around as a mascot. I've called it Ron'. He named his mascot after Ron Noades (1937-2013), a businessman known for his investments in football clubs, who had disparaged Black managers.[314]

**Unease**

Alongside these instances of apparent support, there was unease and agitation. Early in 1970 a Staffordshire branch of the Women's Institute unsuccessfully sought to prevent criticism from the Race Relations Board by reorganising part of their public entertainment: they changed the words of the nursery rhyme 'Ten Little N*gger Boys' to 'Ten Little Golliwog Boys'.[315] Shortly afterwards there was further condemnation of the *Black and White Minstrel Show* and golliwogs but one newspaper reader reacted by writing 'as far back as I can remember, and I'm seventy, we have always had these black-faced entertainers. Why should we change our ways to please people who have come to our country?'[316]

In 1973 controversy of a different kind followed on from a performance of Walsall's St Andrew's Dramatic Society. In *Ritual for Dolls* a box full of Victorian dolls awaken for an hour during

*Opposite page: Products from top left to right, 87a, German Easter Egg with an illustration of a golliwog, early 1900s; 87b, bronze figures of the golliwog and Peg on an alligator, late 1800s or early 1900s; 87c, wallpaper produced by Nutex Wholesalers, c2012; 87d, Cast iron still bank by John Harper, first half twentieth-century; 87e, Clarice Cliff bookend, c1930; 87f hand-painted porcelain beaker, undated; 87g, Royal Doulton figurine of a boy holding a gollywog, c1945-50; 87h, box of Golly Misfitz, a game of 48 cards published by C. W. Faulkner & Co., c1906.*

Golly Misfitz

which time a golliwog attempted to rape the doll Arabella.[317] That year a *Sunday Times* columnist recognised the figure as 'the genesis of colour prejudice in the cradle'.[318]

During the late 1970s and early 1980s the National Committee on Racism in Children's Books, among others, campaigned for a ban. An employee responded to a surge in doll sales following restocking by leading London stores: Ravi Jain complained that instead of being harmless, golliwogs reinforced harmful stereotypes.[319] Golliwog sales had fallen in 1980 to only 2,500 a year whereas up to 200,000 had been annually sold after the Second World War. Two years later it was reported that there was a resurgence in sales including at Hamley's ('they sell very well and we have not had any complaints from the public. Two have reportedly been sold to a Rastafarian couple'). A Robertson's spokesman commented: 'You can't please everyone. No offence is intended. Some people are just looking for trouble.'[320] Public disputes continued. In 1981 a Risley publican named his brown rolls 'Golliwog's Fingers' until a Merseyside community relations worker objected.[321] That year two seventeen-year-olds lost their jobs with a government training scheme in Coventry after they refused to make golliwogs on the grounds of racial discrimination. In 1986 an industrial tribunal heard that a golliwog was hung with a noose at a Birmingham coach station following the departure of a West Indian employee.[322] That year Eddie Chambers, then a Bristol artist, described as 'forceful' in a local newspaper, brought his one-man show, 'The Black Bastard as a Cultural Icon', to Dartington in Devon; in it he explored 'covert racism, the role of the golliwog and other caricatures and explores the hidden meanings behind images that are often superficially regarded by Whites as humorous, inoffensive and innocent'. One of the panels had the autobiographical line 'when I was at school, some of the kids shouted *Get back on your jam jar'*.[323]

The casual usage of golliwog to describe Black men was drawn attention to in 1982 by a columnist who overheard Denis Thatcher, husband of the prime minister, at a Downing Street reception:

> 'You get a lot of these golliwogs rioting and throwing stones at the police and it's all over the television. But as soon as our brilliant police move in and sort them out, there's not a thing about it on television. Do you know why? I'll tell you why. It's because our television people are a lot of pinkoes and closet Marxists. That's why.'[324]

Concerted efforts were made by various local council including in 1983 when Greenwich London Borough Council published *I Love My Golly But…* which outlined in length its objections to the continued use of the golly by Robertson's. Leading political figures had been approached for comment such as Shirley Williams (1930-2021) ('I'm not keen on the golliwog. I am sure its use was innocent enough when it was introduced, but I think is increasingly likely to offend, not least because of the crude abbreviation to w*g') and Enoch Powell (1912-1998) ('I have always thought that to take exception to the use of the golliwog doll is an example of the hysteria over *race relations* which does so much more harm than good').[325] At this time Islington Council banned 'Golly's Cycling Sense', a road safety poster and Merseyside County Council attempted to remove the golly from the International Garden Festival.[326]

That year an exhaust-fitting garage in Birmingham, named Gollywogs Ltd, temporarily removed a sixteen-foot inflatable golliwog from outside its premises. The firm's slogan was 'We don't put jam in jars. We put exhausts on cars'. Next door was ACAFESS (the Afro Caribbean Association for Economic and

Social Security). Its director said:

> 'We have had a neighbourly friendliness with the company but we all wish and pray that one day they will change their name. Black people have their exhausts fitted there and all the mechanics bar one are Black. So, I decided to let sleeping dogs lie rather than get involved in a dispute that could put Black people out of a job'.[327]

For some the debate hinged on whether Britain should accommodate the views of immigrants or if they should accept the status quo. A public debate, which included Bruce Kent and Enoch Powell, was held in 1987 in Buckinghamshire and revealed some of these attitudes. The panel were asked their views on renaming Enid Blyton's 'little black golliwog' to 'little white golliwog'. Sir Alfred Sherman, an influential political writer and analyst, answered that immigrants should be 'grateful for the privilege' of living in Britain and that they should adapt their attitudes towards 'the British way of life'.[328]

## 1990s and the new millennium

In 1988 court martial proceedings revealed that an army corporal had described Black recruits as golliwogs, 'coons' and n*ggers. Such news stories must have contributed to Robertson's decision in 2001 to remove the golly from its advertising. Even so, the firm's action prompted a group of Conservatives serving on Bristol City Council to adopt a golliwog as their mascot. The deputy leader of the council placed a doll in the town hall on the grounds it was nonsense that they were derogatory representations: 'I think it is very sad and the product of a group of people who have got nothing more serious to do'.[329]

In 1991 the public debate on golliwogs focused upon the Gaelic May Day parade in the Scottish town of Peebles. Children had processed in black face perhaps as far back as 1901 but it and the wearing of ten golliwog costumes, owned by the parade committee and stored at the primary school, were banned four months earlier. This caused up to one hundred adults to protest by dressing as golliwogs and blackening their faces.[330] By then the golliwog had been appropriated as a political tool: one doll was 'propped jauntily in a corner' during a General Election interview in 1992 given by Lady Jane Birdwood (1913-2000) for the British National Party.[331]

The arrival of New Labour in 1997 heralded a period in which racial equality and social justice came to the fore of politics. While the golliwog delighted some and, increasingly, disturbed others, few new products were mass produced. Golliwogs became collectable and are now mainly, but not exclusively, the domain of nostalgia collectors rather than of manufacturers. They also found a market as 'Black Americana' or 'Black Memorabilia'.[332] However, they continued to attract controversy such as when in 2009 Carole Thatcher (1953-), the daughter of the former Prime Minister, was dismissed from the BBC after repeatedly describing a Black tennis player as a golliwog. Two years later a Suffolk woman was accused of racially aggravated harassment for displaying a golliwog in her window during a planning dispute with her neighbour of Jamaican heritage. In 2014 a former member of the National Front was imprisoned for twelve months for distributing images intended to stir racial hatred: he had dressed in a Klu Klux Klan costume while hanging a life-sized golliwog doll. Perhaps more significant was a court case in 2013 in which judges decided that the use of the word golliwog in the presence of a Black person was, in itself, tantamount to harassment.

Societal confusion in how to deal with golliwogs is exemplified

*88. West African children with gollywog dolls provided by Gollynomics, 2016.*

by a display of golliwogs in an Essex pub being seized by police in 2023 while only a few years earlier, in 2016, a sixty-five-year-old British woman, who had been born in Ghana, sold golliwog dolls at fairs, school fetes and shows in Hampshire. She dressed as a golliwog and in 2013 started Gollynomics, a 'Bring Golly Back' campaign which funded educational and agricultural projects in Ghana. Charlotte Nightingale believed the doll had travelled from West Africa to the Americas with enslaved women. In what was termed 'reclaiming' her Ghanian heritage, she said 'the doll is now doing amazing things and changing lives'. Her project continued until 2021 by which time approximately £70,000 was raised through the sale of the dolls.

The golliwog continues to be defended, mostly in the tabloid press ('Isn't it time the Golliwog Squad finally grew up?', 'Banned by the BBC… because I was wearing my golliwog',

'Diversity classes at 72 for Tory who said gollies are not racist') and numerous news stories have attracted considerable vitriol.[333] Typical of the many letters of support which continue to be written to newspaper editors was one of 1980 which concluded 'for heaven's sake, please allow us ancient Britons to keep a little of our tradition'.[334] Equally prevalent have been condemnation from commentators who have referred to golliwogs variously as 'the anti-black caricature' (2019), 'a grotesque caricature' (2020), 'non-human and monstrous' (2020) and 'the corrupting caricature' (2021).[335]

The golliwog ebbed away and nearly vanished during the last decades of the twentieth century. A consequence of its demise was the opening of a deep divide in society, part of an avoidance of challenging history such as the British Empire.

*89. English Christmas card by Phyllis Cooper, late 1920s.*

# CONCLUSION

In 1895 American race politics surreptitiously invaded Britain's nurseries and remained there for more than a century. It seeped into the fabric of society. Even so, Britain struggled to recognise that the golliwogg's inspiration, a childhood doll, left America as an anonymous but recognised figure of racial denigration and that it was reborn in Britain as a named humanoid beloved by children who were unaware it had an ethnic identity.

In turn, modern society has failed to grasp that not only did the golliwogg develop incrementally into becoming one of the country's most popular and cherished characters but it was also a pervasive, pernicious and damaging racial stereotype. It did so through the exploitation of the innocence of children. As one writer noted, 'racism takes deepest root when swallowed with mother's milk'.[336]

An American-born daughter of English parents created a character unlike any other in British children's literature. She based it on her own minstrel dandy doll but she fashioned a fairy-tale creature with grey skin and exaggerated Black features. Her figure, however, was not human. Whereas American readers would have readily identified the doll as a racial caricature, British children embraced a character for which they had no cultural or enslavement associations.

Upton's failure to patent her creation allowed other writers, and firms, to appropriate the golliwogg particularly following the publication of her last book in 1909. In doing so they transformed, or returned, her amorphous creature into a

*90. Left: A playing card from 'Golliwogg, A Round Game', c1902.*

recognisable Black man. In the subsequent decades children not only avidly read stories featuring golliwogs but played with them as dolls, were entertained by 'happy-go-lucky darkies' on stage, mimicked them in fancy dress and collected coupons from jam

*91. Below: Cards from the 'Frolicsom Golliwog Snap', undated.*

jars in order to obtain badges.[337] These later generations continued to see, in their childhood innocence, a lovable figure, sometimes a human one, which they treasured.

This continued without interruption until the Caribbean immigration of the 1950s and 1960s when nearly half a million men, women and children changed the ethnic character of Great Britain. One of its consequences was that Britons began to reassess the golliwog. They pondered whether it was an enduring, and powerful, icon of unwitting racism.[338] Over the last two generations the issue was continually and repeatedly debated.

Why was it so difficult for the Edwardians, and for those that came after them, to initially recognise the denigrating and hurtful nature of the golliwog? The evidence clearly shows that from the start the figure's appearance was severely criticised but on the grounds of it being ugly and having a grotesque, that is ungainly, appearance, not for its racial portrayal, although there were instances in which the two were implicitly conflated, consciously or not. It should not be forgotten that those golliwogs produced as good luck charms departed from the minstrel dandy figure. This was due to practicality: it was easier to fashion small hand-made figures to other designs, many of which did not deploy racial stereotyping.

Regarding the waterwog, two reasons help explain the lack of awareness in Devon. First, until recently a miniscule number of Black men and women lived in the county: it is unlikely that they made up as much as 0.1% of the population until the second half of the 1900s. Before this, during the late 1500s and early 1600s, Devon may have had more people of African heritage than most counties. This can be shown in Plymouth and Barnstaple although research has hitherto identified less than fifty individuals across the county in those decades. During the 1700s, 1800s and early 1900s Devon appears to have had isolated individuals rather than a substantial resident Black community. This changed in 1942 when for two years there were high concentrations of Black American servicemen in sporadic locations across the county. In the years immediately after, in the late 1940s and 1950s, few Caribbean immigrants settled in Devon. Even today, the county's ethnicity rates of 92.6% White and 7.4% all others differ substantially from the national rates of 81.7% and 18.3%.[339] Historically, Devonians have had fewer opportunities to become acquainted with people of many other races compared to their urban counterparts in major British cities. But was that reason enough not to question, if not challenge, racial stereotyping as expressed by travelling black-faced minstrels? Not only did these

*92. Family scene, including a golliwog, constructed for commercial advertising, c1949.*

visitors reinforce the perceptions of Black men but Devonians themselves subsequently took to the stage, blacked-up and repeated their performances.

In 1839 a remarkable event took place in Exeter which raises questions on popular perceptions of Black men in more isolated parts of the country. That year a woman asked that Francis Santo, 'the n*gger man', be allowed to kiss her teething infant. He had been incarcerated for begging and the implication is, presumably, that his skin colour somehow gave him supernatural powers. The judges reprimanded the young mother and regretted 'that such ignorance and infatuation should exist in the nineteenth century'.[340]

A second, and greater, factor more easily explains racial attitudes amongst previous generations of British adults: their country's rule over some twenty-five per cent of the world. In 1895, when Upton created the golliwogg, the British Empire was expanding and would not reach its peak for another generation. It is not surprising that people in less-technologically advanced societies were considered unequal by their colonial masters. How else could imperialism be justified? It was said in Exeter in 1963:

> 'Despite disparagement in certain quarters, the building and sustaining of an empire such as we British have known was nothing to be ashamed of. Even with the present exuberance of independence, it should not be forgotten that it was the foresight and toil of past empire builders that has made independence possible'.[341]

It is equally astonishing that this failure to understand the racial implications of golliwogs has continued right up to recent times. On the other hand, the feelings of former children cannot be dismissed as mere nostalgic sentimentality or as grooming in racial stereotyping.

*93. John Bull in a recruitment poster, 1915.*

The absence of corresponding derogatory caricatures of English White men and women may also have contributed to this lack of awareness of the impact of golliwogs upon Black people. The closest figure we have is John Bull, a national personification rather than a racial one. In comparison, longstanding caricatures were made of the Scottish (as parsimonious) and the Irish (as intemperate). During the rise of fascism in the 1920s and 1930s anti-Semitic caricatures were widely disseminated but no single image was pervasive nor was a word specially coined as with golliwogg. Also, whereas blackface was common across the country, whiteface was deployed less often. Devon's only recorded instance of it took place in a location which excluded most Devonians: Dartmoor Prison had the county's only segregated theatre in which Black actors used white makeup.[342]

The golliwog stood alone and apart as a racist caricature. No other non-British character from children's literature, except Teddy, became so overwhelmingly popular and utilised by commercial firms. It is notable that British children did not otherwise clasp dolls depicting subjected people of the Empire with the fervour that they held their golliwog.

The strident criticism in the early 1900s that the character's grotesqueness both damaged children's mental health and perverted British art seems astounding today. It is significant that the sense of 'ugliness' was never directly connected to race but rather to concerns about the golliwogg's misshapen features. His bulk and shock of hair offended those who appreciated only the tidiness of the human form. The two racial stereotyped features, the lips and eyes, were overlooked in this public lambasting and derision. It is telling that some adult observers were baffled by children who not only overlooked physical differences but embraced them. They fell in love with his consistently ebullient, gallant, engaging and well-meaning character. Is it possible to view these children as colour blind either with the grey skin of Upton's golliwogg or the black skin of the revamped golliwog? Equally, it is significant that the adult castigating of the golliwogg ceased once it was revamped more fully in the minstrel dandy tradition.

The recurrent insistence of former children that they were unaware of the golliwog's racial nature is important in the development of British race attitudes. In this, it is crucial to listen to those who owned the soft toy. Equally, those whose lives were adversely impacted by them also need to be heard. As these generations pass it will be more problematic for those in succeeding decades to understand how the golliwog imparted contradictory meanings for a century.

Insensitivity and innocence coincided with the golliwog. The revamping of the golliwogg was an opportunity to remove exaggerated racial features and more accurately portray Black men. The opposite happened. Was this because their appeal amongst British children was centred on them not being

*94. A Robertson's advert of 1932.*

recognisably human? Would a truthful depiction of a Black man not have been as alluring and instead have been considered mundane and dull? Moreover, did the implicit mockery of exaggerated features provide an element of amusement?

*95. An Australian Golliwog doll dressed in a rattan skirt with a floral belt. The necklace and bracelets are made of small scraps of coloured felt. It was made by Ada Perry, an English emigrant to Mirboo North, Australia, c1930-1960.*

The golliwog's imperial expansion added another dimension to its history. The character was enthusiastically received in Australia and New Zealand where the figure became identified not with those of African heritage but to Indigenous people. Polarised debates persist in those countries even as golliwogs continue to be manufactured and sold.

The discovery of an Exeter version of a golliwog presents an opportunity to go beyond modern Britain's focus on debating the figure merely as either an innocent childhood toy or as an icon of racism. In this, all aspects of the wider history of the golliwog demand our understanding. The waterwog brings together some of these threads: it capitalised on childhood appeal, was used as a wartime fundraiser and was created without a racial attribution. It may not have occurred to the Edwardian creators that their bath toy involved a Black man washing clean White skin. Perhaps its importance lies in the few recorded instances made of it. Its

*96. Advertisement for Liver Salts, c1937.*

*97. A hallmarked 9ct articulated golliwog pendant with diamond set eyes, no date.*

creation was not considered surprising or particularly remarkable. It was representative of the ubiquitous nature of the golliwog by 1914 and possibly an indication of other as-yet-unrecorded British examples.

This returns us to the golliwog's extraordinary popularity amongst all social groups and to how its original incarnation later diverged. The golliwog was highly visible not only as a literary character and wartime amulet but in fancy dress, fundraising events and on stage and car bonnets. The wider perspective raises other difficult questions. Why did this figure become the leading good luck charm of the Great War? How does that square with (White) Britain's perceptions of Black men and women then and now?

*98. A French golliwog measuring some 90 cm in length, undated.*

For a modern audience, several decades after the dropping of the golly, the golliwog and golliwogg have lost some of their visual racial sting; they have become largely irrelevant to the younger generation. American nineteenth-century minstrel dandy clothing no longer resonates as it did when performers routinely appeared in blackface; such ostentatious clothing is no longer recognisable as caricature. Other racial signifiers are also less potent. Blubber lips are now more likely to be identified with cosmetic enhancement rather than with racial denigration. Furthermore, the golliwog's bubble mass of hair is no longer seen as exclusively Black. Only the over-sized staring eyes remain perplexing as to an implied meaning.

Britain continues to have marked social divisions over ethnicity. The golliwog's long and contested history, in all its divergent strands, provides society with an opportunity to look more closely, and recognise not only that this is challenging and awkward history but one which is nuanced and multi-dimensional. Race is likely to be a pivotal social issue for generations to come. It is for this reason that a candid appraisal of the contradictory golliwog has to be made before we can fully appreciate and understand its place in British society.

The storyline of *Golliwog*, a film which was released as *Tomorrow at Ten* (1963), provides a useful analogy with the innocence with which many children played with their golliwogs: in it a child is presented with an innocuous golliwog doll not knowing it has been weaponised and is in reality a time bomb. In both instances children subsequently learn that the golliwog has troubling associations for adults.

The golliwog represents a Britain which has passed. A germane example of this is the Nignog Club, a social enterprise for school children run by a North of England chain of newspapers from 1929 until at least 1951. It was initially intended that girls would be called nigs and boys would have the name nogs but the editor changed his mind and implored children to rejoice *We are going to be Nignogs! Nignogs!! Nignogs!!!*[343] This language, shocking in modern Britain, is more complex than is generally remembered. The term 'nignog' has two meanings: the more recent one is well-known as an offensive term to describe dark-skinned people but the earlier definition was 'a new or unskilled recruit; a novice; a foolish or naive person'. It is similar to another North of England slang word; ning-nong defines 'a fool, a stupid person'.[344] In 2002 the *Lancaster Guardian* excused Jim Bowen, a presenter at BBC Radio Lancaster, for using nignog in a broadcast for its modern

*Products from top left to right, 99a, baby carriage biscuit tin, marked 'the United Co-operative Baking Society Ltd, Glasgow, Clydebank & Belfast, with a decoration of a golliwog, undated; 99b, wallpaper featuring golliwogs, 1920; 99c, golliwog-decorated record player, c1930.*

meaning but he protested it was meant as local dialect.[345]

At one point the golliwog was used to entice children into joining this social club but this link was coincidental. The Nignog Club had no racial overtones. For many apparent reasons, this terminology, as well as the word golliwog, have to be used carefully and sensitively but, first of all, they need to be understood in their present and past contexts. Without that knowledge, it would be possible to unconsciously give offence as well as make connections where there were none.

The golliwogg originated 130 years ago as a legacy of enslavement in former British colonies. It is an example of cultural appropriation albeit one which had unforeseen consequences. The golliwogg successfully embedded itself into British culture but its racial nature was not noticed until the ethnic character of Britain fundamentally changed in the middle of the twentieth century. Since then the golliwog has divided public opinion even as the figure has become irrelevant to the younger generation. Memories of it are fading but at its very heart the golliwog retains the ability to raise searching questions as well as teach some hard lessons about the development of multi-cultural Britain.

History is never exclusively about the past, it is no more than that which is viewed, recognised and evaluated through a modern lens. The golliwogg, golliwog and golly bear witness to this.

# ILLUSTRATION SOURCES

**Cover**, front, privately supplied; back, 1, privately supplied, 2, Ladenbuger Spielxeugauktion, 3, Florence Upton, *The Adventures of Two Dutch Dolls and a 'Golliwogg'* (London, 1895), p23

**Frontispiece** & **2**, Florence Upton, *The Adventures of Two Dutch Dolls and a 'Golliwogg'* (London, 1895), p23 & p49; Victoria & Albert Museum, B.50-2010; **1**, *The War Illustrated,* 22 Dec. 1917, p363; **3** & **4**, Edith Lyttelton, *Florence Upton, Painter* (London, 1926), facing p9 & p19; **5**, Library of Congress, POS - MIN - U5, no. 9, C size, P&P; **6**, Victoria & Albert Museum, B.493-19977; **7**, Thomas Hood, *The Comic Annual* (London, 1839); **8-10**, Library of Congress, 2012647237, 2022631986 & 2001700597; **11**, the artwork appears in Upton's books listed in endnote 42; **12**, Wellcome Collection, 2043302i; **13**, *Punch*, 10 Nov. 1920; **14**, Fowl, *The First Book of Eve* (New York, 1916), p47; **15**, Library of Congress, POS-TH-1899.U53, no. 7; **16**, *The Graphic*, Christmas Issue, 1913; **17**, State Library Victoria PCTAF 295; **18**, Metropolitan Museum of Art, 08.242; **19**, Bertha Parker Hall, *Ducky Daddles' Party* (New York, 1918), p19; **20**, *Father Tuck's Annual* (London, date unknown); **21,** C. Fraser-Simson, *The Adventures of Golly Smith* (London, 1956); **22**, Ruth Ainsworth, *Rufty-Tufty The Golliwog* (London, 1952); **23**, Wolf Mankowitz, *Majollika and Company* (London, 1955); **24**, *Gollywog Picture Book* (New York, 1955); **25** *Little People's Annual* (London, date unknown); **26**, *The Chummy Book* (1924); **27**, May Byron, *The Adventures of Dumpy Dimple and His Dog!* (New York, 1908); **28**, Louis Robbins, *Dutch Doll Ditties* (London, 1904); **29a**, privately supplied; **29b**, Locati Auctions, 14 Nov. 2021, lot 1121146; **29c**, Hawleys Auctioneers, 20 Feb. 2021, lot 207; **29d**, Dominic Winters Auctions, 15 Dec. 2017, lot 480; **29e-g** & **30a-c**, privately supplied; **30d**, International Military Antiques; **30e**, Vectis Auctions Ltd, 28 Aug. 2018 lot 5503; **30f**, privately supplied; **30g**, Hakes Auctions, 22 March 2012; **30h**, privately supplied; **30i**, Milestone Auctions, 28 May 2016; **30j**, privately supplied; **30k**, Reeman Dansie Auctions, 13 Oct. 2021, lot 2442; **30l**, Langston University; **30m-n**, Hakes Auctions, 21 Jan. 2010; **30o**, Copake Auction Inc., 18 Feb. 2017; **30p**, Ladenbuger Spielxeugauktion; **31a**, *Dumfries & Gallo-*

*way Standard*, 13 Oct. 1909; **31b**, *Orcadian*, 19 March 1910; **32**, Museums Victoria, 1899759; **33**, Bernie Grant Trust, Grant/2/15/4; **34**, *Pinto's Panto or Round-About Tales* (London, 1926); **35**, *Sheffield Evening Telegraph*, 3 Feb. 1915; **36**, *Leicester Daily Mercury*, 9 Feb. 1915; **37**, *Lancashire Evening Post*, 23 April 1915; **38**, *Yorkshire Evening Post*, 1 April 1915; **39**, Wellcome Images, EPH/66/14; **40**, Eastbourne Auctions, 10 Dec. 206, lot 2343; **41**, Jerry Loader, *The Folly of the Golly*, p91; **42-3**, privately supplied; **44**, Bernie Grant Trust, Grant/2/15/1; **45**, Wellcome Images, EPH/66/12; **46**, Bernie Grant Trust, Grant/2/15/7; **47**, Northeastern University Library, Archives and Special Collections, M89, Box 7; **48**, privately supplied; **49**, hhtp://www.tuckdbpostcards.org; **50**, *Ten Little Gollywogs*, (?London, 1909); **51a-b**, hhtp://www.tuckdbpostcards.org; **51c**, Newberry Library, NL112VE2; **51d**, hhtp://www.tuckdbpostcards.org; **52a**, Simpson Galleries, 6 March 2016, lot 546; **52b-c**, privately supplied; **52d-e**, Vectis Auctions Ltd, 5 July 2005, lot 2454 & 16 May 2007; **53**, *Advocate*, 21 Jan. 1930; **54a-b**, Newberry Library, NL112VDR & NL112V3; **54c-d** hhtp://www.tuckdbpostcards.org; **55a-b**, privately supplied; **55c**, Bonhams Auctions; **55d**, privately supplied; **55e**, Morphy Auctions, 9 Nov. 2014; **55f**, privately supplied; **55g-i**, Locati Auctions; **55j**, privately supplied; **55k**, Soulis Auctions, 7 Dec. 2008; **55l**, Morphy Auctions, 24 Sept. 2016, lot 182a; **55m-p**, privately supplied; **56**, *Green Left Weekly* 841, 19 June 2010; **57**, J. A. Bentham, Shoes (London, 1923); **58**, *Philadelphia Inquirer*, 12 Nov. 1904; **59**, New England Auctions, 16 Oct. 2021, lot 161; **60**, privately supplied; **61**, *The Minneapolis Morning Tribune*, 8 June 1963; **62**, Unilever Archive of Unilever, GB1752.UAC/1/11/9/44/5; **63**, State Library Victoria, 1793521; **64**, Mitchell Library, State Library of New South Wales, 85658; **65**, Museums Victoria, MM 2298; **66**, State Library, New South Wales, 20293; **67**, the artwork appears in Upton's books listed in endnote 42; **68**, *Bystander*, 8 March 1905; **69**, hhtp://www.tuckdbpostcards.org; **70**, National Library of Australia, MUS Snell N mba 786.44 D943; **71**, Bernie Grant Trust, Grant/2/15/18; **72-3**, Library of Congress, 2016745260 & 2016791039; **74**, Eastbourne Auctions, 27 Nov. 2020; **75**, hhtp://www.tuckdbpostcards.org; **76**, privately supplied; **77**, the artwork appears in Upton's books listed in endnote 42; **78**, hhtp://www.tuckdbpostcards.org; **79**, Temple University, Special Collections Research Center, PT080827; **80**, Carole Haines; **81-2**, hhtp://www.tuckdbpostcards.org; **83**, Elmwood Players; **84**, State Library of Queensland, 27189; **85**, Spielzeugmuseum/Toy Museum Nuremburg; **86**, Joe Mills; **87a**, Ruby Lane; **87b**, privately supplied; **87c**, Nutex Wholesalers Ltd; **87d**, Bertoia Auctions, 11 Nov. 2016, lot 607; **87e-f**, privately supplied; **87g**, Pascoe & Co.;

**87h**, The World of Playing Cards; **88**, Gollynomics; **89**, hhtp://www.tuckdb-postcards.org; **90**, Beinecke Rare Book and Manuscript Library, 10686738; **91**, The World of Playing Cards; **92**, National Science and Media Museum, 1997-5002_10754; **93**, Library of Congress, 2003675386; **94**, *The Children's Newspaper*, 24 Sept. 1932; **95**, Museums Victoria, HT 2901; **96**, Antikbar, 22 April 2017; **97-8**, privately supplied; **99a**, Bertoia Auctions, 11 Nov. 2017; **99b**, Victoria & Albert Museum, E.2378-1983; **99c**, Locati Auctions, 19 Nov. 2023

# REFERENCES


1 H. G. Wells, *The Holy Terror* (London, 1939), p140; *A G. K. Chesterton Omnibus* (London, 1936), p307; Aldous Huxley, *Two or Three Graces* (New York, 1926), p275; E. M. Forster, *Howards End* (New York, 1951), p94; E. F. Benson, *Queen Lucia* (New York, 1920), p65; James Joyce, Ulysses (New York, 1984 edn), p760; Elinor Glyn, *Romantic Adventure* (London, 1936), p294; Aldous Huxley, *Aldous Huxley's Stories, Essays and Poems* (Letchworth, 1923), p82; Carl Anthony, *As We Remember Her* (New York, 2003), p18; *Cincinnati Enquirer*, 30 Aug. 1981; Mini Rhea, *I was Jacqueline Kennedy's Dressmaker* (New York, 1962), p56.

2 *The Wide World Magazine* 117 (Aug. 1956), p262.

3 *Daffodils and Narcissi* (Kidderminster, 1911), pp5 & 16.

4 C. G. Grey, *A History of the Air Ministry* (New York, 1940), p47; *Daily Mirror* (Sydney), 1 Nov. 1944; *Catholic Freeman's Journal*, 2 Feb. 1939; *Nottingham Journal*, 27 Oct. 1945; *Daily Advertiser* (Waga Waga), 9 Jan. 1951; *The Children's Newspaper*, 11 Dec. 1956; *The American Kennel Club Stud Book* 34 (New York, 1917), p1007. The Blue Golliwog was a chow chow; *Ruff's Guide to the Turf* (London, 1920), p375; In 1919 R. Floyd Clarke, a lawyer of New York, owned *Golliwog*, a yacht. He was the descendant of wealthy planters from South Carolina: *Dilatory Domiciles July 1919* (Social Register Assoc., 1919), p647 & John William Leonard (ed.), *Who's Who in Finance and Banking* (New York, 1922), p137. The Australian cow was the property of P. C. Taylor: *The Journal of the Department of Agriculture Victoria* 50 (Victoria, 1952), p571. The Gloxinia was named in the early 1970s: *The Gloxinian* 26 (1976), p3; *Doubt* 2: 33 (1931), p82.

5 *Biggleswade Chronicle*, 28 Sept. 1973.

6 *The People*, 17 June 1979.

7 *Dundee Courier*, 24 Sept. 1990.

8 *Dundee Courier*, 24 Sept. 1990; *Birmingham Post*, 15 June 1996.

9 Olga Buttigieg, *Recognising the spirituality of the Golliwogg: an analysis of Upton's Golliwogg picture books* (Australian Catholic University doctoral dissertation, 2014).

10 *Toronto Daily Star*, 2 May 1916.

11 *Daily News*, 7 June 1919; *Sheffield Independent*, 10 Sept. 1920.

12 *Exeter & Plymouth Gazette*, 26 Aug. 1921; *Staffordshire Advertiser*, 28 Nov. 1914; *Thanet Advertiser*, 9 Dec. 1916; *Prestatyn Weekly*, 14 March 1914 & 4 April 1925.

13 Todd Gray, *Voices of Empire in Exeter* (Exeter, 2024), I, pp37-8; *Common Cause*, 22 Jan. 1915; *Western Times*, 28 Nov. 1914, 1 & 6 Dec. 1914, 2 Oct. & 24 Nov. 1915; *Exeter & Plymouth Gazette*, 18 Nov. 1914; Owen Davies, *A Supernatural War* (Oxford, 2018), pp160, 169, 171; U.K. Census, 1911, Exeter.

14 *London Evening Standard*, 30 April 1980. See Gillian Klein, *Reading into Racism* (London, 1985), pp41-2. Hot water bottles decorated with golliwogs were for sale in 1967: *Chemist and druggist* (28 Oct. 1967), p11.

15 Todd Gray, *Voices of Empire in Exeter* (Exeter, 2024), I, pp37-8; *Tribune* (19 March 1943), p15.

16 *The Colac Herald*, 19 June 1908; Edith Lyttleton, *Florence Upton, painter* (1926), p10; Davis, *Lark*, p11; *The Scotsman*, 10 Oct. 1930; *The Children's Newspaper*, 13 Jan. 1951; *Westminster Gazette*, 14 Sept. 1907; *Herts & Essex Observer*, 3 Sept. 1965; Lesley Gordon, *A Pageant of Dolls* (New York, 1949), p35; *Coventry Evening Telegraph*, 19 Dec. 1963.

17 *Playthings* 94:11 (Nov. 1996).

18 *Pall Mall Gazette*, 23 Nov. 1899; *Hampshire Telegraph*, 14 March 1908.

19 Mamie Meredith, 'Negro patois and its humor', *American Speech* 6:5 (June 1931, pp317-318; Ernest Weekley, *A Concise Etymological Dictionary of Modern English* (New York, 1952), p179; Christopher Howse, 'A word echoing with an uncomfortable caricature, and God', *Daily Telegraph*, 5 Feb. 2009.

20 *East Kent Times*, 12 Nov. 1965; *Londonderry Sentinel*, 21 June 1927; *Daily Mirror*, 30 March 1977.

21 *Denbighshire Free Press*, 4 Sept. 1909; *Cincinnati Enquirer*, 4 July 1909.

22 *Daily Telegraph & Courier*, 4 Oct. 1895.

23 *The Journal of Education* 42:21 (28 Nov. 1895), p371.

24 *Times of India*, 22 Nov. 1902.

25 *The Churchman* 86 (July – Dec. 1902), p689; *The Nation*, 5 Dec. 1901; *The Christmas Bookseller* (1896), p46.

26 *The Review of Reviews* 18 (1898), p611; *Sporting Times*, 2 Dec. 1905; *The*

*Queen*, 15 Dec. 1900; *Birmingham Daily Gazette*, 16 Nov. 1904; *Globe*, 13 Dec. 1905 & 14 Dec. 1904; *Graphic*, 7 Nov. 1903; *Nottingham Guardian*, 24 Oct. 1903; *Westminster Gazette*, 15 Oct. 1901; *Sheffield Independent*, 19 Oct. 1898; *The Delineator* 65 (1905), p142; *Evening Mail*, 12 March 1917.

27 *Bookseller*, 25 Dec. 1907.

28 'Some Holiday Books', *The Kindergarten Magazine and Pedagogical Digest* 19 (1906-1907), p295

29 *The Sunday Times*, 8 Sept. 1895.

30 *The Christmas Bookseller* (1900), p71.

31 *London Daily Chronicle*, 31 July 1929; *Sussex Daily News*, 16 March 1917; Marilynn Olson, 'Turn-of-the-Century Grotesque: The Upton's Golliwogg and Dolls in Context' *Children's Literature* 28 (2000), p74; *The Morning Star*, 5 Nov. 2021; *Daily Mail*, 5 Feb. 2009; Victoria & Albert Museum, B.493.1997.

32 *Morning Advertiser*, 3 Jan. 1834. In contrast, Upton had purchased herself the Dutch dolls which she admitted to a journalist, 'One day on the way from school she chanced by a penny shop where toys were sold. Some wooden jointed dolls caught her candy and she bought them. From these models she drew illustrations.': Adaline D. Piper, 'Florence K, Upton, Painter', *The American Magazine of Art* (1923), pp487-8.

33 *Observer*, 29 Nov. 1846.

34 *Observer*, 17 Feb. 1839.

35 *The Scotsman*, 25 Sept. 1874. It was published in Australia the following year: *Rockhampton Bulletin*, 9 Jan. 1875.

36 *Guardian*, 6 Dec. 1888. The book was written by J. G. Sowerby and published by George Routledge & Sons.

37 *South London Observer*, 13 July 1889.

38 *Newry Telegraph*, 30 Aug. 1862.

39 David Rudd, *Enid Blyton and the Mystery of Children's Literature* (London, 2000), p139.

40 William Chambers, *Things as they are in America* (Philadelphia, 1854), p355; Harold Beaver, 'Time on the Cross: White Fiction and Black Messiahs', *The Yearbook of English Studies* 8 (1978), p42; *New York Times*, 24 June 1895; Todd Gray, *Not One of Us* (Exeter, 2018), pp258-9; *Guardian*, 24 May 1969.

41 *Western Times*, 11 Oct. 1895; *Exeter Flying Post*, 14 Dec. 1895; *Western*

*Morning News*, 21 Sept. 1881.

42 *The Golliwogg's Bicycle Club* (1896), *The Golliwogg at the Sea-side* (1898), *The Golliwogg in War!* (1899), *The Golliwogg's Polar Adventures* (1900), *The Golliwogg's 'Auto-Go-Cart'* (1901), *The Golliwogg's Air Ship* (1902), *The Golliwogg's Circus* (1903), *The Golliwogg in Holland* (1904), *The Golliwogg's Fox-hunt* (1905), *The Golliwogg's Desert Island* (1906), *The Golliwogg's Christmas* (1907), *The Golliwogg in the African Jungle* (1909).

43 'Editorial Comment', *Collier's* 51:2 (1913), p13.

44 Rudd, *Blyton*, p169; *Daily Mirror*, 11 March 1907.

45 *Sunday Sun*, 17 April 1921.

46 *Daily Record*, 9 Jan. 1960.

47 William Rose Benet (ed.), *The Reader's Encyclopedia* (New York, 1948), p444.

48 *Times of India*, 31 Oct. 1931.

49 *Belfast Telegraph*, 23 Jan. 1953.

50 *Daily Mirror*, 2 Aug. 1977; *The South African Pioneer*, May 1908 & August 1910.

51 *The Sun* (Sydney), 8 Oct. 1950.

52 *Sunday Times*, 24 Aug. 1997; *Newsday*, 24 May 1972; *The Sun* (Vancouver), 24 Aug. 1964; *Teen* 9:6 (June 1965); Jerry Bowles, *A Thousand Sundays* (New York, 1980), p185; Roy Pickard, *Shirley MacLaine* (New York, 1985), p56; Michael Freedland, *Jack Lemmon* (London, 1985), p87; *Shipley Times,* 18 Dec. 1957; *The Observer*, 21 Dec. 1958; *Sunday Post*, 9 Dec. 1979; *Birmingham Daily Post*, 10 April 1996; Andrew James Caine, *Interpreting Rock Movies* (Manchester, 2004), p123; Ben H. Bagdikian, FBI file, p23, quoting *Time Magazine*; *America: A Catholic Review of the Week* 69:19 (14 August 1943), p522; *Burton Observer*, 10 Feb. 1972; *Belfast Telegraph*, 20 Nov. 1979; *Playboy* 18:4 (April, 1971), p150.

53 William Wallace Campbell, *East Africa by Motor Lorry* (London, 1928), p246; Baden Powell, *Scouting Round the World* (London, 1935), pp35-6; P. H. Sparks, 'Gurkhas climb Borneo's Highest Mountain', *Journal of the United Service Institution* LXXVII: 326 (Dec. 1947), p317; *Financial Post* 53:3 (Jan. 17 1959).

54 *Portsmouth Evening News*, 23 Jan. 1959.

55 Lyttelton, *Florence Upton*, pp8-10.

56 Norma S. Davis, *A Lark Ascends* (Metuchen, 1992), p10.

57 *Good Housekeeping* XXXVI (January to June, 1903), p465.

58 *Hampshire Telegraph*, 14 March 1908.

59 Davis, *Lark*, pp18-19; *Black & White*, 3 Dec. 1904.

60 *Sporting Times*, 11 Nov. 1905.

61 *Truth*, 21 Dec. 1905.

62 *Times*, 6 Dec. 1895.

63 *Dundalk Examiner*, 13 Dec. 1913; Janet Erskine Stuart, *The Education of Catholic Girls* (London, 1914), p105; *The Times*, 4 Dec. 1913.

64 *Airdrie & Coatbridge Advertiser*, 3 Aug. 1912.

65 *Gloucester Journal*, 24 June 1916.

66 *Sunday Mail* (Brisbane), 16 Aug. 1931.

67 Haidee Wright, 'The gollywog and the cult of ugliness', *Vanity Fair, January – June 1916* (Ann Arbor, 1966) p71.

68 *London Daily Chronicle*, 19 July 1929; 'Editorial Notes', *The Nursing Times* 25:1265 (27 July 1929), p869; *Manchester Guardian*, 4 Jan. 1928.

69 *The Telegraph* (Brisbane), 19 Dec. 1936.

70 *London Daily Chronicle*, 31 July 1929.

71 *Daily Telegraph & Courier*, 17 Nov. 1896.

72 *The Toronto Daily Star*, 9 Nov. 1901.

73 David Rudd, 'Upton, Florence Kate (1873-1922)', *Oxford Dictionary of National Biography* (Oxford, 2004); *Birmingham Daily Gazette*, 21 Oct. 1901; *South Devon Weekly Express*, 22 Oct. 1909.

74 *Black & White*, 24 Nov. 1900.

75 Edgar Osborne, 'The Birth of Golliwog', *The Junior Bookshelf* 12:4 (Dec. 1948), p160.

76 *Biggleswade Chronicle, 30 March 1928; West of England Advertiser*, 27 Dec. 1929; *Runcorn Weekly News*, 23 Dec. 1926; *Gloucester Citizen*, 27 Feb. 1935; *Sunday Mirror*, 25 Dec. 1936; *Bookseller*, 22 May 1935; *Daily Mirror*, 18 Jan. 1937; *The Stage*, 31 Dec. 1954; David Rudd, *Enid Blyton and the Mystery of Children's Literature*, Univ. of Sheffield doctoral thesis (1997), p221, p226.

77 *Grimsby Daily Telegraph*, 30 Aug. 1980; Davis, *Lark*, pp103-104. Robertson's used the gollywog at least by 1915: *Evening Despatch*, 18 June 1915; *Dundee Evening Telegraph*, 7 Feb. 1910.

78 *Truth*, 2 Dec. 1955.

79 *London Evening Standard*, 26 Feb. 1957.

80 *Bury Free Press*, 20 Feb. 1970; *Nottingham Evening Post*, 15 Feb. 1964.

81 *Daily Mail*, 3 Dec. 1965.

82 *The Sunday Times*, 11 April 1971.

83 *Liverpool Daily Post*, 16 Nov. 1972; *Daily Mirror*, 24 March 1975.

84 *Daily Mirror*, 1 Jan. 1987; *Daily Express*, 1 Jan. 1987; *Sunday Independent* (Dublin), 22 April 1990; *Bristol Evening Post*, 3 Aug. 1990; *Western Daily Press*, 5 Oct. 1990; *Newcastle Journal*, 15 Oct. 1990; Robert Macgregor, 'The appropriation of a commercial trademark; the golliwog as a cultural marker', *Children's Folklore Review* 33 (2011), p51.

85 Rudd, doctoral thesis, pp249-52.

86 Olga Buttigieg, *Recognising the spirituality of the Golliwogg: an analysis of Upton's Golliwogg picture books* (Australian Catholic University doctoral dissertation, 2014), pp199-224; *Yorkshire Evening Post*, 13 May 1915.

87 Rudd, *Blyton*, pp132-54; Sally Tomlinson, *Education and Race from Empire to Brexit* (Bristol, 2019), p44; *Pearson's Weekly*, 18 Dec. 1901; *Lambert's Family Almanack* (1911), pp6-7.

88 *Gentlewoman*, 1 Dec. 1900; *Dundee Courier*, 22 June 1908; *Evening Irish Times*, 27 Oct. 1905; *Manchester Evening News*, 20 Dec. 1957.; *East & South Devon Advertiser*, 10 Nov. 1906; *Evening News*, 24 Aug. 1912. The Doulton figure was called Golliwog and was made in the late 1940s: *Catalog of Copyright Entries: Works of Art, Reproductions of Works of Art, Scientific and Technical Drawings, Photographic Works, Prints and Pictorial Illustrations* 1:7-11a:1 (Washington 1947), pp151, 185.

89 University of Exeter Main Library, Electronic Resources, The Transformation of Shopping, File 04: journals and magazines, 1941-1962; *Daily Telegraph* (Launceston), 17 Dec. 1927; *Philadelphia Inquirer*, 20 Dec. 1923; *St Louis Post-Dispatch*, 21 Oct. 1923.

90 *The Soda Fountain* 29 (July 1924), p92; *National Hotel Review* 18 (Jan. – April 1924), p67.

91 *The Herald* (Melbourne), 11 Oct. 1927.

92 *Wellington Times*, 21 Jan. 1915. In 1903 Germany produced the brass buttons for English golliwogs: *Gloucester Journal*, 4 July 1903.

93 *Evening Mail*, 20 Aug. 1919.

94 Loader, *Folly*, p66; *Telegraph*, 8 Dec. 2008 & 11 Feb. 1996.

95 *West Gippsland Gazette*, 20 April 1909. He also bought a golliwog at a toyshop in Cowes: *The Star*, 13 Sept. 1909.

96 *Daily Express*, 8 Aug. 1918; Ann Morrow, *The Queen Mother* (New York, 1985), p42; *Daily News,* 9 July 1921; *Hartlepool Northern Daily Mail*, 24 Nov. 1922; *Punch* 246:6439 (5 Feb. 1964); *Weekly Dispatch*, 26 Dec. 1926; *New York Times*, 16 Dec. 1928; *Daily Express*, 8 Dec. 1979; *Vancouver Sun*, 12 Dec. 1936; *Queensland Figaro*, 17 Sept. 1927; *Western Champion* (Parkes), 26 April 1928; *Yorkshire Post*, 17 Oct. 1932; *The Sun* (Sydney), 19 Dec. 1945; *The Scotsman*, 8 Nov. 1935; *Belfast News Letter*, 20 July 1955; *Weekly Dispatch*, 9 June 1957; *The Times*, 8 July 2008; *The Herald* (Melbourne), 26 Sept. 1939.

97 *Newsweek*, 9 Aug. 2017. The Royal association even extended to golliwogs decorating the first-class nursery onboard the *Queen Mary* in 1936: *The Sydney Morning Herald*, 20 Feb. 1936.

98 *The Sunday Times*, 11 April 1971.

99 *Daily Record*, 4 March 1913; *Daily Mirror*, 2 Jan. 1913; *Evening News* (London), 2 Jan. 1913; *The Orcadian*, 19 March 1910; *Dundee Evening Telegraph*, 30 Jan. 1914; *Londonderry Sentinel*, 3 Jan. 1914; *Yorkshire Evening Post*, 13 May 1915; *Buchan Observer*, 12 Oct. 1909. See in Robert M. MacGregor, 'The Golliwog', pp124-32; in Sammy R. Danna (ed.), *Advertising and Popular Culture* (Bowling Green, 1992).

100 *Geelong Advertiser*, 3 July 1912; *The Tatler*, 14 April 1920 & 13 Oct. 1926; *Punch* 169:4424 (26 Aug. 1925) & 242:6349 (16 May 1962); *Edinburgh Evening News*, 20 May 1936; *Picture Post* 3:4, 29 April 1939; Unilever Archive, GB1752.SDC/62/2/111/151; *Picture Post* 48:1, 1 July 1950; *Good Housekeeping* 65:5 (1 Nov. 1954); *Picture Post* 32:3, 20 July 1946 & 33:5, 2 Nov. 1946; *Hartlepool Northern Daily Mail*, 17 Nov. 1962; *Scunthorpe Evening Telegraph*, 30 Aug. 1980.

101 *Daily Mail*, 3 Aug. 1966.

102 *Pinto's Panto or Round-About Tales* (London, 1926), pp6, 124-5.

103 *Daily News*, 7 Dec. 1927; *The Sun News* (Melbourne), 25 Oct. 1927; *Leicester Evening Mail*, 11 Sept. 1922; *Birmingham Daily Post*, 18 July 1961 & 14 Nov. 1963; Adrian Smith, '*The Yellow Teddybears*: exploitation as education', in Kate Egan, Martin Ian Smith and Jamie Terrill (eds), *Researching Historical Screen Audiences* (Edinburgh, 2022), p166. The alleged school was never identified.

104 *Proceedings of the World Forum on Syphilis and other Treponematoses* (Washington, 1962), p361; David McGillivray, *Doing rude things* (London, 1992), p54. In contrast, in 1919 'the Gollywog's Control', Anatole

France's satire on birth control, was performed in New York: *Theatre Magazine* 30: 221 (July 1919), p83.

105 *Kensington Post*, 12 Dec. 1969.

106 *Airdrie & Coatbridge Advertiser, 3 Aug. 1912; Acton Gazette*, 7 Dec. 1951; *Chronicle* (Adelaide), 24 Jan. 1914; *Selfridges Christmas Catalogue* (1962), item 353/54; *Birmingham Mail*, 2 May 1903.

107 *Hearth and Home* XVIII: 448 (14 Dec. 1899); Walton-Sears Mail Order Catalogue (1958). He was advertised in 1954 as 'dressed in blue trousers, red jacket, white collar and a resplendent black belt with tie ends. He has a fine mop of shaggy black hair.': *The Mail* (Adelaide), 6 March 1954.

108 Personal communications with the Hain Daniels Group, 21 & 27 August 2024; Loader, *Folly*, pp115, 118-119. To date I have been unable to locate any company records or discussion of them.

109 The firm claimed that it began using the golliwog in 1910 but no adverts have yet been found before 1915. David Newton, *Trademarked* (Stroud, 2008), pp165-6; *Nottingham Evening Post*, 4 Feb. 1915; *East Kent Times*, 12 Nov. 1965; *Belfast News-Letter*, 26 Nov. 1976; *Aberdeen Press*, 25 Nov. 1978; *Edinburgh Evening News*, 7 Dec. 1961; *Grimsby Evening Telegraph*, 19 May 1984; *Derby Daily Telegraph*, 13 Oct. 1992; *Guardian*, 27 Aug. 2001. By 1956 Robertson's claimed it had been using the golliwog for over fifty years: *Maclean's* 69:4 (18 Feb. 1956), p42; *Financial Times*, 4 Dec. 1961. Jerry Loader believed that William Robertson had travelled in the United States: Loader, *Folly*, p20, 59. Canada has also been suggested as the country where Robertson 'discovered' the golly: Stanley Sacharow, *Symbols of Trade* (New York, 1982), pp67-8. Robert Opie thought Robertson's began using the golly as its trademark in 1914: Robert Opie, *The Art of the Label* (London, 1987), p92.

110 *Financial Times*, 8 Nov. 1961 & 3 Dec. 1969.

111 *Chester Chronicle*, 2 Oct. 1943; *Southern Reporter*, 13 Nov. 1924.

112 Loader, *Folly*, p79; *Manchester Evening News*, 20 April 1934; *Guardian*, 24 April 1936; *Sydenham, Forest Hill & Penge Gazette*, 16 Nov. 1951.

113 *Grimsby Daily Telegraph*, 30 Aug. 1980; Univ. of Exeter, Electronic Resources, Market Research & American Business, 1935-1965, pilot motivational research on Robertson's mincemeat, Feb. 1961, p13.

114 *Daily Express*, 21 Dec. 1959; *Edinburgh Evening News*, 7 Dec. 1961; *Newcastle Journal*, 8 May 1964; *The Scotsman*, 24 June 1966; *Manchester Evening News*, 2 Dec. 1969; *Aberdeen Press*, 24 Aug. 1974; *Sunday Express* 6 Aug. 1978.

115 *Staffordshire Sentinel*, 9 Sept. 1927; *Motherwell Times*, 8 June 1928; Lane Demas, *Game of Privilege* (Chapel Hill, 2017), p31.

116 *Edinburgh Evening News*, 6 Nov. 1935; *Daily Telegraph* (Sydney), 7 Aug. 1939.

117 *Lynn Advertiser*, 23 Aug. 1955.

118 UK Civilian Aviation Authority, serial number 196; *Staffordshire Sentinel*, 20 July 1976; *Sheerness Times*, 1 Aug. 1975; *Birmingham Daily Post*, 29 Dec. 1976; *Manchester Evening News*, 11 July 1979; *London Evening Standard*, 20 June 1975; *Coventry Evening Telegraph*, 24 June 1974 has details of the earlier 65 feet high balloon; Loader, *Folly*, p90-4, 100.

119 Loader, *Folly*, p95; *Eastbourne Gazette*, 7 Nov. 1973; *Eastbourne Herald*, 10 Nov. 1973; *Daily Express*, 26 Oct. 1985; *London Evening Standard*, 25 Oct. 1985.

120 *Guardian*, 4 May 1975 & 18 Sept. 1983; *The Economist*, 25 June 1983; Loader, *Folly*, pp95, 100, 107. See Clare Francis, *Come Hell or High Water* (London, 1994 edn), p5, 15-16, 26; Nick Faldo, *Faldo, in search of perfection* (London, 1997).

121 *Daily Mirror*, 17 March 1967.

122 *Western Times*, 15 Feb. 1936.

123 *Times*, 24 Dec. 1993; *Daily Telegraph*, 23 Aug. 2001.

124 *Times*, 8 & 18 Oct. 1962. The executive producer was Ronald H. Riley and the writer and director was Richard Taylor.

125 *Daily Mirror*, 30 April 1968; British Film Institute, 750756 & 750854. Adanac Productions was the productions company. The producer was Barbara Kelly.

126 *Daily Mirror*, 30 April 1968; *Telegraph*, 8 May 1968.

127 *Western Daily Press*, 29 July 1972; *Daily Mirror*, 31 Oct. 1972. See also *Liverpool Echo*, 19 March 1973.

128 *Bookseller*, 11 June 1977; *Wolverhampton Express & Star*, 31 Dec. 1982; *Grimsby Daily Telegraph*, 30 Aug. 1980; Jan Nederveen Pieterse, *White on Black* (New Haven, 1992), pp156-7; *Daily Telegraph*, 23 Aug. 2001; *Pittsburgh Press*, 31 Oct. 1982.

129 *Daily Telegraph*, 20 May & 30 Oct. 1984; *Times*, 1 May 1984; *Liverpool Echo*, 2 May 1984; *Guardian*, 1 May 1984.

130 *Manchester Evening News*, 30 July 1984.

131 *Daily Telegraph*, 21 May 1984.

132 *Manchester Evening News*, 30 July 1984; *Daily Telegraph*, 20 Oct. 1982.

133 *Manchester Evening News*, 30 July 1984; *Daily Telegraph*, 20 Oct. 1982.

134 *Times*, 24 Aug. 2012 & 23 Aug. 2001. For an account of the issue up to 1984 see 'The press, the jam jar and the gollywog', *Searchlight* 111 (Sept. 1984), p16.

135 Marilynn Olson, 'Turn-of-the-Century Grotesque' p73 in *Children's Literature* 28 (2000).

136 Lyttleton, *Florence Upton*, p12; Olson, 'Turn', pp79-81.

137 It is not known whether her childhood books had the positive depictions of Black men and women which could be found in the first half of the nineteenth century: J. R. Oldfield, 'Anti-Slavery sentiment in children's literature, 1750-1850', *Slavery & Abolition* 10:1 (1989), pp44-59. For a later romance between a golliwog and a doll see R. Helps, *Nobody Loves Me* (London, 1950).

138 *Alfreton Journal*, 4 Jan. 1907; *Reading Standard*, 20 Feb. 1909; *Hunts County News*, 21 May 1925; *Newark Advertiser*, 31 Oct. 1934; *Liverpool Echo*, 5 Jan. 1935.

139 Davis, *Lark*, pp108-110; *The Children's Newspaper*, 13 Jan. 1951; Susanne Reichl, 'Articulating Cultural Meanings: The Example of the Golliwog(g)', pp169-70 in Marie Hologa, Christian Lenz, Cyprian Piskurek & Stefan Schlensag (eds), *Cases of Intervention: The Great Variety of British Cultural Studies* (Cambridge, 2013).

140 *Luton Reporter*, 27 Dec. 1915; *Melton Mowbray Times*, 10 Nov. 1922; *Derby Daily Telegraph*, 16 Jan. 1924.

141 *London Daily Chronicle*, 17 Dec. 1923.

142 *Westminster Gazette*, 17 June 1927 & 16 Jan. 1928; *Sheffield Independent,* 24 Dec. 1928; *Daily Mirror*, 14 March 1934; *Peterborough Standard*, 2 Jan. 1953.

143 *Daily Herald*, 12 July 1919; *Spalding Guardian*, 18 Oct. 1940.

144 *The Australasian*, 14 Feb. 1920.

145 *Bury Free Press*, 9 March 1940.

146 *Redcliff Review*, 11 Sept. 1930.

147 *Yorkshire Factory Times*, 18 May 1916. In 1909 an Australian wrote a children's story which explained that the golliwog had been White but became Black in order to scare other creatures: *The Catholic Press*, 28 Oct. 1909.

148 *Pontypridd Observer*, 24 April 1969. For a similar story, see *The Mail* (Adelaide), 22 April 1950.

149 *Westminster Gazette*, 14 Sept. 1907; *Jerilderie Herald & Urana Advertiser,* 29 Nov. 1907.

150 M. Gehrts, *A Cinema Actress in the Wilds of Togoland* (Philadelphia, 1915), pp75-6.

151 *Daily Mirror*, 28 Nov. 1908.

152 *The Sunday Times*, 21 Jan. 1917.

153 Anne Olivier Bell (ed.) *The Diary of Virginia Woolf*, 1931-1935 (London, 1982), IV, p210.

154 *Times of India*, 20 March 1925; *Dundee Courier*, 19 Sept. 1922; *Richmond Herald*, 11 June 1910; *Nottingham Journal*, 15 Dec. 1936; *Nelson Leader*, 4 Jan. 1946; *The Australasian*, 30 Jan. 1943; *Alderly & Wilmslow Advertiser*, 25 Sept. 1953; *Fifeshire Advertiser*, 13 Nov. 1948; *Lewisham Borough News*, 2 May 1933. In 1941 an Australian newspaper reported that the word originated during the First World War: an officer who served in Palestine in 1917 claimed that because the Arabs resented the names given to them by the Australians and order came through from general headquarters that 'all ranks must refer to the Arabs as Worthy Oriental Gentlemen: *Smith's Weekly*, 22 Feb. 1941 & *Richmond River Herald*, 29 Aug. 1941. Another letter-writer recalled its use from about 1927 in the Punjab: *The Argus*, 1 March 1946. In 1916 Senegalese and Arab patients in a French military hospital were referred to as black golliwogs: *Common Cause*, 1 Dec. 1916.

155 *The Times Educational Supplement*, 23 Nov. 1956.

156 *Staffordshire Sentinel*, 5 June 1943; *Derby Daily Telegraph*, 10 Nov. 1977. It has also been widely claimed that 'ghul, the term for Egyptian workers, was added to w*g to make up the term 'golliwog': *Sunday Sun*, 22 May 1994.

157 *Weekly Dispatch*, 24 April 1949.

158 *Daily Mail*, 1 July 1964.

159 *Southern Morning Herald*, 22 Sept. 1923; *The Sun News* (Melbourne), 2 Oct. 1924; *The Sun* (Sydney), 21 Jan. 1940; *Mirror* (Perth), 16 May 1942; *The Daily News* (Perth), 16 May 1951.

160 *Staffordshire Sentinel*, 5 Sept. 1942. Another soldier wrote at this time that the term was used by servicemen: *Bo'ness Journal*, 8 May 1942. It was also used amongst the military in India: *Liverpool Echo*, 29 July 1942.

161 *The Bioscope*, 16 Nov. 1916; J. A. Bentham, *Shoes* (New York, 1923).

162 Lionel James, *The History of King Edward's Horse* (London, 1921), p188; See also Denis Mackail, *Bill the Bachelor* (Cambridge & New York, 1922),

p79; Dorota Flatau, *Yellow Souls* (New York, 1918), p128 and Roland Grimshaw, *Indian Whirlpools* (London, 1928), p29.

163 *Western Daily Press*, 20 June 1917.

164 Winston Churchill, *My Early Life* (1930), p156.

165 *Daily Mirror*, 5 Dec. 1932.

166 Wolverhampton City Archives, DX-624/6/29.

167 *The Scotsman*, 20 July 1977.

168 Michael Baptiste, 'Ignoring NHS racist abuse does not make it go away', *Mental Health Practice* 25:4 (7 July 2022), p7.

169 Robert Macgregor, 'The Appropriation', pp53-4.

170 Esther Lawson, *Wogamatter* (London, 2016), p79.

171 *Leicester Daily Mercury*, 13 Feb. 1995.

172 *The Observer*, 4 Nov. 2001; *New York Daily News*, 23 June 2008.

173 *The Sphere*, 23 June 1928.

174 *The Cologne Post*, 12 Dec. 1919.

175 *Sheffield Independent*, 8 Oct. 1919; *The Herald* (Melbourne), 8 March 1945; *Newsweek* 25:10 (5 March 1945). The French had an aberrant association: the code word the United States Navy used in the Second World War for the Free French was golliwog: Dorothy E. Richard, *Glossary of U. S. Naval Code Words* (Washington, 1948 edn), p15; *New York Times*, 20 May 1923.

176 *Western Times*, 20 July 1918.

177 *B. Shackman & Company Favors and Novelties* (New York, 1912), p70; *San Francisco Chronicle*, 22 Nov. 1912.

178 *The Globe & Mail* (Toronto), 20 Dec. 1965. This origin was also claimed in 1930: *The Sunday Times*, 13 April 1930; *Leicester Chronicle*, 25 Feb. 1966. In 1967 another toymaker produced Albert and Ginge, two toys which reportedly looked like white golliwogs: *Kentish Express*, 22 Sept. 1967.

179 *The Queenslander*, 14 Oct. 1882; *St Nicholas* IX:11 (Sept. 1882).

180 *Harper's Bazaar* 50 (1915), p112.

181 *Exhibitors' Herald World* (22 Feb. 1930), p54.

182 *Exhibitors' Herald World* (10 March 1928), p46.

183 *Newsweek* 3:1 (6 Jan. 1934), p19; *Cleveland Call & Post*, 3 Feb. 1938; *Pittsburgh Courier*, 11 Feb. 1933; *Philadelphia Tribune*, 7 Feb. 1935; *New York Tribune*, 30 Nov. 1919; *Detroit Free Press*, 19 June 1979; *The Michigan Alumnus* 33 (1927), p565. *Philadelphia Inquirer, 12 Nov. 1904; St Louis Post-*

*Dispatch*, 18 June 1989; *Good Housekeeping* 66:5 (1 Nov. 1954); *The Hartford Courant*, 6 June 1926;

184 *Motion Picture* (June 1924), p106.

185 *Hollywood* (Nov. 1942), p55; Roy Moseley, *A life with the Stars* (Sevenoaks, 1988), pp117-118; Thierry de Navacelle, *Sublime Marlene* (New York, 1984), p28; David Bret, *Marlene my friend* (London, 1993), p48.

186 *Newsday*, 10 Jan. 1961; *Cincinnati Enquirer*, 16 July 1962, 9 Aug. 1970 & 16 Sept. 1973. The copyright was allegedly held by Etta Mansfield. See *Official Gazette of the United States Patent Office* 248 (October, 1917), p508.

187 *Newsweek* 70:3 (17 July 1967).

188 *Hartford Courant*, 10 June 1999. See also 17 May 2000 & 8 Jan. 2001 for similar projects with different schools.

189 *Philadelphia Inquirer*, 5 April 1962 & 29 Oct. 1963; *Minneapolis Star*, 10 Sept. 1965; *Minneapolis Morning Tribune*, 17 Jan. 1964; *Chicago Tribune*, 20 Jan. 1968. They began to close in 1972: *Minneapolis Star*, 21 Sept. 1972; *Toronto Star,* 28 May 1966 & 6 March 1973; *The Sun* (Vancouver), 11 March 1969. John Denver was familiar with the Golliwog Lounge in Minneapolis: Leonore Fleisher, *John Denver* (New York, 1976), p46.

190 Charles Suhor, *Jazz in New Orleans* (Lanham, 2001), pp37, 176.

191 *Daily Mirror*, 24 Aug. 1966.

192 'Odds and Ends', *The Wide World Magazine* 6 (Oct. 1900 – March 1901), p102.

193 *Toronto Daily Star*, 9 Nov. 1901.

194 *Cincinnati Enquirer*, 24 Oct. 1909.

195 *The Eastern Province Herald*, 17 Nov. 1905 & 20 Dec. 1906; *Southern Rhodesia Handbook* (London, 1914), p64; *Rand Daily Mail*, 21 Oct. 1909; *The Katoomba Daily*, 13 Nov. 1936; *The Daily Telegraph* (Sydney), 15 Feb. 1936; *The Rhodesia Herald*, 28 Dec. 1906; *Cape Times*, 14 Oct. 1912.

196 *Rand Daily Mail*, 16 Dec. 1910.

197 *Newsday*, 11 May 1995.

198 *Children's Newspaper* 1660 (13 Jan. 1951); *Nottingham Evening Post*, 22 March 1950; *Petersburg Times*, 24 Aug. 1894; *Western Mail* (Perth), 14 April 1894.

199 *The Herald* (Melbourne), 15 Oct. 1936; *Werribbee Shire Banner*, 6 Oct.1938; *The Mercury* (Hobart), 19 Sept. 1938; *The Children's Newspaper*, 19 Nov. 1938.

200 *Smith's Weekly*, 25 July 1936.

201 *The Mail* (Adelaide), 27 Aug. 1938; *Bendigo Advertiser*, 5 July 1909; *Punch* (Melbourne), 21 May 1915.

202 *Advocate* (Tasmania), 13 March 1954.

203 *The Skipton & Streatham Gazette*, 3 Nov. 1923.

204 *The Telegraph* (Brisbane), 8 Dec. 1923; *The Daily Telegraph* (Sydney), 24 April 1928.

205 *The Catholic Advocate*, 4 Dec. 1930.

206 Dale Collins, *Sea-tracks of the speejacks round the world* (New York, 1923), p61; Fergus Hume, *The Green Mummy* (New York, 1908), pp33-4; *The Herald* (Melbourne), 27 May & 18 Dec. 1943.

207 *Brisbane Times*, 7 June 2024; *Sunday News* (Auckland), 30 Oct. 2022; *The Border Mail*, 5 March 2024; Donna Leslie, 'Loved and Despised: Imagining the Golliwog Doll in the Australian Context', *Journal of Australian Indigenous Issues* (2018).

208 *The Bystander*, 5 Aug. 1914.

209 Lyttleton, *Florence Upton*, p14; Olson, 'Turn', p80. In 1963 Mrs Phyllis Robinson, former receptionist to Miss Upton, recalled the golliwog was used as a plaything while children had their portraits painted: Margaret Hutchings, *Dolls and How to Make Them* (London, 1970 edn), p149.

210 *Holloway Press*, 25 Feb. 1898; *The Times*, 28 Nov. 1910.

211 *Dundee Evening Telegraph*, 14 April 1938; *Liverpool Echo*, 20 April 1963.

212 *The Sun News Pictorial* (Melbourne), 29 April 1936. He appeared in blackface in *Swing Time*: *Shields Daily Gazette*, 2 Oct. 1936.

213 *The Bystander*, 8 March 1905; *The Observer*, 27 Nov. 1910; *Kinematograph Weekly*, 31 Dec. 1908, 7 Jan. 1909 & 23 Nov. 1916; *Bolton Evening News*, 23 Dec. 1913; *Lancashire Evening Post*, 3 June 1913; Newton Lee, *Disney Stories* (New York, 2012), p49.

214 *East End News*, 9 April 1909; *Reading Standard*, 24 April 1909.

215 *Eastern Counties Times*, 18 Nov. 1910.

216 *Queensland Figaro*, 3 Sept. 1932; *Table Talk*, 26 Feb. 1920.

217 *Sheerness Guardian*, 6 June 1908; *Leicester Chronicle*, 14 Oct. 1922.

218 *The Sunday Sun*, 18 March 1906.

219 *Women's Life* 439 (7 May 1904).

220 Andre Castaigne, *The Bill-Toppers* (Indianapolis, 1909), p227. An example of actors who kept golliwogs was Michael Plinge who in 1975 kept in

his dressing room a two-inch golliwog given to him by his mother on his first night in rep: Richard Huggett, *Supernatural on Stage* (New York, 1975), p90.

221 *Sunday Post*, 18 April 1926.

222 *Daily Mirror*, 17 Feb. 1914.

223 *Lincolnshire Echo*, 7 June 1919.

224 *Western Mail*, 27 Sept. 1927; Ann McKinley, 'Debussy and American Minstrelsy', *The Black Perspective in Music* 14:3 (Autumn, 1986), p249; *Western Morning News*, 13 Feb. 1926.

225 *The Wednesday Era*, 14 May 1913.

226 *The Era*, 28 April. 1906; *Newcastle Journal*, 26 Nov. 1963.

227 *Essex Times*, 22 Jan. 1913; *Islington Gazette*, 22 Sept. 1909; *Southern Echo*, 1 Sept. 1910; *The Era*, 13 Feb. 1909; *South London Observer*, 29 Jan. 1908; *Northern Whig*, 6 Feb. 1913; *Luton Reporter*, 27 Dec. 1915; *Chester Chronicle*, 18 March 1916; *The Stage*, 3 Feb. 1916; *Beverley Independent*, 14 Jan. 1905; *London & Provincial Entr'acte*, 6 July 1906; *Blackpool Gazette & Herald*, 16 July 1907.

228 *Sunday Mirror*, 10 Dec. 1916.

229 Imperial War Museum, L.R. 127.2.

230 *Islington Gazette*, 18 Nov. 1909; *Gravesend & Northfleet Standard*, 20 Jan. 1911; *Caerphilly Journal*, 20 May 1922 & 1 Dec. 1934.

231 *The Age*, 31 July 1915.

232 *Herne Bay Press*, 20 Sept. 1913.

233 *Advocate* (Melbourne), 3 Sept. 1953.

234 *Daily News* (London), 22 Dec. 1910.

235 Golliwog charms were still being sold in 1940: *The Tatler*, 29 Nov. 1950.

236 *Guardian*, 3 Sept. 1903; *Bournemouth Graphic*, 7 Dec. 1917; *Football Gazette*, 12 Sept. 1908; *Exeter & Plymouth Gazette*, 9 Sept. 1909; *Weston-Super-Mare Gazette*, 15 June 1910; *Nottingham Journal*, 30 June 1913; *The Times*, 22 July 1914. The Golliwog Dance was invented by Will Bishop in 1896: *Morning Leader*, 15 Jan. 1909.

237 *Western Mail* (Perth), 4 March 1926. It was also termed 'a Congo Golliwog': *Dundee Courier*, 9 Sept. 1932.

238 *The Herald* (Melbourne), 26 Feb. 1920.

239 *San Francisco Chronicle*, 16 Aug. 1908.

240 *Evening Standard*, 20 Sept. 1928; *Yorkshire Evening Post*, 10 Dec. 1917;

*Wallacefield Christmas Book* (1 Dec. 1917), pp30-2. A poem was written in 1917 entitled 'The Gollywog Craze': Imperial War Museum, B.R.C.S. 26.2/5.

241 *Aldershot News*, 12 July 1907.

242 C. Lewis Hind, *Life and I* (London, 1923), p140-4; *New York Tribune*, 6 Jan. 1924.

243 *Western Morning News*, 16 Dec. 1922.

244 *Bromley & West Kent Mercury*, 22 July 1927; *Perthshire Advertiser*, 9 June 1928; *Crediton Gazette*, 23 June 1923; *Torbay Express*, 18 May 1929.

245 *West Sussex County Times*, 17 May 1924.

246 *Guardian*, 10 June 1925.

247 *News (Adelaide)*, 4 Nov. 1930.

248 *North Devon Journal*, 5 Jan. 1922; *Western Morning News*, 3 Jan. 1923.

249 *Western Gazette*, 8 Oct. 1926.

250 *Exeter & Plymouth Gazette*, 1 Feb. 1929; *Tiverton Gazette*, 12 Oct. 1926; *Exeter & Plymouth Gazette*, 18 April 1947, 6 Feb. 1925, 23 Jan. 1926.

251 *East Kent Times*, 21 April 1920.

252 *The African Standard*, 22 Oct. 1910.

253 *Western Morning News*, 24 Dec. 1923.

254 *Western Times*, 8 Jan. 1926; *Mafeking Mail*, 25 April 1923.

255 *The Sun* (Sydney), 29 July 1927.

256 *Tiverton Gazette*, 7 March 1922; *Exeter & Plymouth Gazette*, 3 May 1924; *Lincolnshire Echo*, 16 Dec. 1938.

257 *Birmingham Daily Gazette*, 19 April 1920.

258 *Manchester Evening News*, 31 May 1926.

259 *Guardian*, 22 Aug. 1925.

260 *Croydon Times*, 18 July 1923.

261 *The Stage*, 18 April 1929; *The Graphic*, 7 Sept. 1929.

262 *Anaconda Standard*, 25 April 1921.

263 John Galsworthy, *The Little Man and Other Satires* (New York, 1915), p61.

264 *South Bank Express*, 4 Nov. 1922; *Yorkshire Post*, 23 Feb. 1925; *Daily Record*, 23 Feb. 1925

265 *Weekly Dispatch*, 12 Dec. 1920; *Daily Mirror*, 13 Nov. 1918; *Sunday Sun* (Newcastle), 14 Oct. 1928. In 1913 it was suggested that it was then the Age of Golliwogs because of the ugliness of toys: *Bradford Daily Telegraph*, 4 Dec. 1913.

266 *North Devon Journal*, 24 July 1930.

267 *Coleshill Chronicle*, 19 Jan. 1957; The window was designed by Nora Yoxall and Elsie Whitford in 1928 but not installed until 1933. I am grateful to Carole Haines for this information.

268 *Daily Express*, 2 April 1938; *Liverpool Echo*, 7 Feb. 1948.

269 *Western Morning News*, 12 Oct. 1940, 10 Sept. 1943; *Exeter & Plymouth Gazette*, 24 Dec. 1941.

270 *Food Manufacture* xxxi:8 (1946), p366.

271 *Western Morning News*, 15 Dec. 1949.

272 *Guardian*, 17 Dec. 1931.

273 *Guardian*, 4 March 1925.

274 *West Sussex Gazette*, 10 April 1952; *Junior Bookshelf* 16:2 (1952); *Lancashire Evening Post*, 23 April 1959; *The Spectator* 214: 7145 (4 June 1965); *Punch* 237:6219 (2 Dec. 1959); Ann K. McClellan, 'Golly, A Black Sherlock Holmes!: Race, Cross-Promotion and Robertson's Golliwog' 53:1, *The Journal of Popular Culture* (Feb. 2020), pp10-33.

275 *Manchester Evening News*, 7 Nov. 1958; *London Evening Standard*, 30 July 1962.

276 *Sunday Mirror*, 3 July & 30 Sept. 1955.

277 There was a second house named The Golliwogs in 1955: *Birmingham Daily Post*, 26 April 1955.

278 *Belfast Telegraph*, 26 Oct. 1954; *Esher News & Mail*, 20 Nov. 1959; *Northern Whig*, 10 Feb. 1955. This firm was at 679 Stratford Road in Sparkhill: *Warwickshire Kelly's Directory* (1972-3), p986 & *Birmingham Mail*, 29 Jan. 1969.

279 *Hampshire Telegraph*, 9 Dec. 1955.

280 *Somerset Standard*, 24 Nov. 1933.

281 *London Evening Standard*, 11 May 1957; *The Tatler*, 5 Nov. 1958.

282 *Birmingham Weekly Post*, 26 Oct. 1956.

283 *The Children's Magazine*, 22 Nov. 1958.

284 *Grimsby Daily Telegraph*, 9 Aug. 1957. Ten years later Joe Orton wrote 'What the Butler Saw' in which white golliwogs were mentioned 'She's making white golliwogs for sale in color-prejudice trouble spots': Lesley Hazleton, *England, Bloody England* (New York, 1990), p61.

285 Chris Bentley, *The Complete Gerry Anderson: The Authorised Episode Guide*

(London, 2008 edn), pp16-21.

286 Angela Rodaway, *A London Childhood* (London, 1985), pp26-7.

287 *Leeds Mercury*, 8 Dec. 1928.

288 *Coventry Standard*, 14 Nov. 1958.

289 *Nottingham Guardian*, 6 Oct. 1958.

290 *Leicester Chronicle*, 25 Feb. 1966.

291 *Conversations With a Golliwog, A Play by Alexander Guyan* (London, 1963).

292 British Film Institute, 38806.

293 *Daily Mirror*, 28 May 1964; *Crewe Chronicle*, 7 March 1964.

294 *Liverpool Daily Post*, 10 April 1965.

295 *Walsall Observer*, 3 Nov. 1967; *Wolverhampton Express*, 19 Oct. 1967.

296 *North Wales Weekly News*, 4 Dec. 1969.

297 *Fabulous 208,* 16 Jan. 1971; *Hartlepool Northern Daily Mail*, 23 Sept. 1961; *Cumbernauld News*, 14 Sept. 1962; John Fogerty, *Fortunate Son* (New York, 2015), p104.

298 *Kelly's Western Mail Directory* (London, 1967), p282; *South Wales Echo*, 28 March 1991.

299 *The Observer*, 7 Nov. 1965; *Bury Free Press*, 9 Dec. 1960.

300 *Derby Daily Telegraph*, 1 Jan. 1966; *The Globe & Mail* (Toronto), 20 Dec. 1965; *The Observer*, 7 Nov. 1965. In 1965 the *Financial Times* reported 'the golliwog still survives, despite doubts about it racialist undertones': *Financial Times*, 12 Nov. 1965.

301 *Middlesex County Times*, 19 Sept. 1964.

302 *Daily Record*, 19 May 1967; *Wolverhampton Express & Star*, 27 Aug. 1968.

303 *Daily Mercury*, 14 May 1968.

304 *Daily Express*, 23 April 1969.

305 'Golliwog in Exile', *Punch* 186:4868 (21 March 1934); *Halifax Evening Courier*, 16 July 1938; *Hindustan Times*, 9 July 1940. It was also claimed in 1936 that golliwogs in Italy were being destroyed because they were Ethiopian: *The Uralla Times*, 27 Feb. 1936.

306 *Weekly Dispatch*, 28 June 1959.

307 *Wolverhampton Express*, 20 April 1970; Geoffrey Beattie, *We Are The People* (London, 1993), p103; *Rugby Advertiser*, 23 April 1971. The author was Paula K. Bell.

308 *Financial Times*, 8 Oct. 1971.

309 *Worthing Gazette*, 28 July 1971.

310 *Sunday Post*, 6 May 1973.

311 *Birmingham Mail*, 11 Jan. 1974.

312 *Torbay Express & South Devon Echo*, 10 June & 19 July 1982.

313 *Wolverhampton Express and Star*, 23 Aug. 1983; 'April Golly', *New Society* (4 April 1985); *London Evening Standard*, 2 Feb. 1990. See also *Daily Telegraph*, 7 Feb. 1990.

314 *Wales on Sunday*, 10 Nov. 1991.

315 *Daily Mirror*, 13 April 1970.

316 *Western Daily Press*, 29 July 1972; *Daily Mirror*, 31 Oct. 1972. See also *Liverpool Echo*, 19 March 1973.

317 *Walsall Observer*, 23 Feb. 1973.

318 *The Sunday Times*, 14 April 1974.

319 *Bookseller*, 11 June 1977; *Wolverhampton Express & Star*, 31 Dec. 1982; *Grimsby Daily Telegraph*, 30 Aug. 1980; Jan Nederveen Pieterse, *White on Black* (New Haven, 1992), pp156-7; *Daily Telegraph*, 23 Aug. 2001; *Pittsburgh Press*, 31 Oct. 1982.

320 *Times*, 20 Aug. 1981; *Daily Telegraph*, 20 Oct. 1982; *Sunday Mirror*, 17 Oct. 1982.

321 *Runcorn Guardian*, 2 Jan. 1981.

322 *Coventry Evening Telegraph*, 18 Aug. 1981; *Birmingham Mail*, 16 April 1986.

323 *Torbay Express & South Devon Echo*, 26 Feb. 1986; Eddie Chambers, 'Blackness as a Cultural Icon', *TEN.8* 2:3 (Birmingham, Spring, 1992), pp126-7.

324 *Punch* 6391 (5 May 1982).

325 *Birmingham Post*, 1 May 1984; Laila Coleman, *I love My Golly But…* (London, 1985).

326 *Telegraph*, 20 May & 30 Oct. 1984; *Liverpool Echo*, 2 May 1984.

327 *Birmingham Mail*, 31 Aug. 1987; *The Guardian*, 9 June 1988.

328 *Buckinghamshire Advertiser*, 7 Jan. 1987.

329 *Daily Telegraph*, 17 May 1988 & 23 Aug. 2001; *Birmingham Daily Post*, 15 June 1996; *Daily Mail*, 22 June 1999; *Halifax Evening Courier*, 28 Aug. 2001; *Shropshire Star*, 5 Sept. 2001; *Guardian*, 6 Sept. 2001.

330 Macgregor, 'The Appropriation', pp54-7.

331 David Rudd, *Enid Blyton and the Mystery of Children's Literature*, Univ. of

Sheffield doctoral thesis (1997), p221. In 2009 a twelve-year-old girl burned a golly in a bonfire at a 'fun day' of the British National Party. It followed a mock trial of Winston who was charged with 'mugging, rape, drug dealing': *News of the World*, 23 & 30 Aug. 2009.

332 Clinton Derricks-Carroll, *Buy Golly!* (2005); Francis Joseph (ed.), *The Golly Collectors Handbook* (London, 2003); Dee Hockenberry, *Collecting Golliwoggs Teddy Bear's Best Friends* (Atglen, 2003). Merrythought last manufactured golliwog dolls but ceased production in 2011. See www.gollybadges.com, for instance, for modern manufacturing. Collectables are sold through various sites including www.golligosh.co.uk, www.golliwog.co.uk, www.gollycorner.co.uk and www.gollyland.co.uk.

333 *Daily Mail*, 6 Feb. 2009, 10 Jan. 2015, 21 Dec. 2013; *The Times*, 6 Feb. 2009; *Guardian*, 8 Sept. 2011 & 11 April 2023; *Ghana Guardian*, 28 August 2016; *Daily Mail*, 27 Aug. 2016; *Times*, 27 Aug. 2016; *Guardian*, 8 Jan. 2014; Macgregor, 'The appropriation', pp51-63; information supplied by personal communication with Charlotte Nightingale, 3 & 5 Dec. 2024.

334 *The Times*, 3 June 1980.

335 Maisha Wester, *Twenty-first-century Gothic* (Edinburgh, 2019), p299; Chinua Thelwell, *Exporting Jim Crow* (Amherst, 2020), p194; Rebecca Wanzo, *The Content of Our Caricature* (New York, 2020), p63; Brannon Costello, *Keywords for Comics Studies* (New York, 2021), p195. See Donna Varga & Rhoda Zuk, 'Golliwogs and teddy bears: embodied racism in children's popular culture', *Popular Culture* 46: 3 (June 2013); *The Times*, 19 Dec. 2013.

336 *The Guardian*, 27 Aug. 2001.

337 *Guardian*, 7 Feb. 2009.

338 *The Times*, 22 Nov. 2013.

339 Todd Gray, *Devon's Last Slave-Owners* (Exeter, 2021), pp129-38.

340 Todd Gray, *Not One of Us* (Exeter, 2018), pp256-7.

341 *Express & Echo*, 8 Aug. 1963.

342 Gray, *Devon's Last Slave-Owners*, p243.

343 *Morecombe Guardian*, 5 Nov. & 7 Dec. 1929, 27 April 1934. *Lancaster Guardian*, 28 Sept. 1951; Frank Howard Timperley also organised the formation of a women's cricket league: *Bradford Observer*, 11 June 1948.

344 *Oxford English Dictionary*.

345 *Lancaster Guardian*, 11 Oct. 2002; *The Visitor*, 31 Dec. 2002.

# INDEX

Abolition **49**

Acland, Richard 139

Adams, Marcus 62

Afghanistan 97

Africa 12, 30, 32-3, 40, 67, 78, 85, 95, 104, 123, 156, 173, 179; East Africa 42; East Africa Turf Club 143; Ethiopia 205 n305; Ghana 168; Mafeking 143; Mombasa 143; Nigeria **117**, 153, 162; North 109; Senegal 109, 198 n154; South Africa 94, 111, 117, 143, 159; *South African Pioneer* 40; Sudan 46; Swaziland 40; Togoland 93; West Africa 97, 168; Zimbabwe 116-117

Ainsworth, Ruth 149

air pilots 12, 135

Allen, Joe 106

animals 19, 30, 46, 122; cow 12, 188 n4

art, effect on 47-8

Askey, Arthur 125

Astaire, Fred 125-6

Atkins, Thomas 94

Atkinson, Rowan 41

Aunt Sally 32-3

Australia 12, 25, 40, 62, 65, 67-8, 76, 95-7, **118-119**, 120-23, 129, 133, 135, 140, 158, 179, 188 n4, 190 n35, 197 n147, 198 n154; Adelaide 120; Brisbane **121**, 158; Geelong 119; Golliwog Bachelor Club 120; Golliwog Lady 120; Golliwogs Social Club 120; Indigenous people 121; Kooloonog **121**; Queensland 122; Sisters of Nazareth Orphanage 133; Sydney **121**; Victorian Golliwog Club 120

Bannerman, Helen 88

Baptiste, Michael 105

Beamish, Pat 153

Beat Generation 42
Beatles 41
Bedfordshire 12; Luton 87
Belgium 17
Benson, E. F. 11
Berkshire 151; Reading 127
Berry, W. H. 129
Bideford 142
Birdwood, Jane 167
Birmingham 13, 133, 144, 152; ACAFESS 165; coach station 164; football 133; garage 165; Sparkhill 204 n278
Birtles, Francis **119**; Nea **119**
Bishop, Will **126**, 202 n236
*Black and White Minstrel Show* 7, 21, 100, 152, 156, 162
Black, Cilla 153-5
Blackpool 62, 149
Blyton, Edith 51-5, 84, 100, 149, 166
Borneo 42
Botha, Pik 118
Bow Belles **39**
Bowen, Jim 182-3
Boy Scouts 143
Boyce, A. F. 119-120
boyliwog 26
Braden, Bernard 78
Bristol 72, 102, 140, 164; City Council 166
British Broadcasting Corporation 21, 104, 156, 167-8, 182; Radio Lancaster 182
British Empire 14, 21, 23, 104, 108-109, 116-23, 133, 137, 149, 152
British National Party 167, 207 n331
British Rail 65
Brittain, John 146; Vera 146
Bromell, J. 142
Buckinghamshire 166

Bull, John **176**

Cambridgeshire, Peterborough 88
Campbell, Naomi 106
Canada 48, 90, 116, 195 n109; Niagara Falls 116; servicemen 17; Toronto 17, 116
cards, birthday **128**; Christmas **84**, **86**, **89**, **98**, **170**; cricket **137**; German 142; patriotic **134**; playing **172**; postcards **85**; rocking **148**
Caribbean, the 21, 65, 104-5, 120, 149, 152, 173-4; Barbados 104-105; Jamaica 130, 152, 167; Montserrat 106; Trinidad 106
Carroll, Lewis 28
Chambers, Eddie 164; William 33
Chapman, Harold **38**
Cheshire, Alsager 155; Crewe 155
Chesterton, G. K. 11
China 117, 143
Christmas 28, 44, 51, 62, 84, **86**-7, **89**, **98**, 133, 143, 146, 150, 156, **170**; tree 146
Chudleigh 161
Churchill, Winston 96
Clark (Clarke), Mollie 149; Sam 12-13
Clausen, George 47
Collins, Jose 129
Connolly, Cyril 94; Jean 94
Constantine, Learie 106
Cooper, Gunner 142
Cornwall 161-2
cricket 106, 132, **137**, 207 n343; Lord's 106

Dali, Salvador 41
dandies **33**, 34, 63-5, 86, 171, 173, 177, 181
Dartington 164
Dartmoor Prison 176
Davis, Bette 115
De Gaulle, Charles 109

Debussy, Claude 11, 129
Denver, John 200 n189
Derbyshire, Derby 87, 133, 153; Risley 164
Designer & Art Association 80
Devon 14, 19, 37, 144, 146, 161, 164, 173-6; population 173-4
Di Melfi, Giuseppe 135
Dietrich, Marlene 115
Dodd, Ken 40
dolls **8**, 27, **30**, 37, 46-7, 66, 90, **101**, 102, 108-9, 121, 144, **145**, 155, **179**, 207 n332; African 46, 168; Australian 123; Black 31-2, 37, 54, 66, 111, 119; Chinese 66; Dutch **24**, 27-8, 48, 55-6, 68, 83, 85, 116, 146, 190 n32; European 66; French 113, 140; gender 67-8; German 60, 103, 159; Indigenous American 66; Japanese 66; making 19, 66-7; Mammy 111-112; Mary Anne 112; Mr Smith 111; Nenette 109; rag 12, 14, 24, 27, 70, 115-117, 119, 133; Rintintin 109; sizes 67-8; Suzy 68; talking 130; White 91, 94, 119; wooden 26; yarn 109, 113, **118** see golliwogs
Dylan, Bob 41

East Sussex, Eastbourne 75
Egypt 95, 97, 120, 143, 198 n156; loofah 18
Einstein, Albert 41
Eisenhower, Dwight D. 12
Emmett-Dunne, Mia 151
Essex, Hornchurch 146; public house 168
Exeter 17-20, 34, 37, 102, 109, 127, 133, 142, 175, 179; bishop 146; collar factory 18; Gaumont Theatre 146; Heavitree 127; High Street 17; Higher Summerlands 19; Palace Gate 18; Prisoners of War Fund 146; Topsham 133; War Relief Committee 17-18; Wreyford & Son 37
exhibitions, British Toy Manufacturers 156; Children's Illustrated Books 62; Commonwealth 63; Grocers and Allies Trades 73; International Garden Festival 79; Lincolnshire & Norfolk Dairies 74-5

Faldo, Nick 76
Festival of Britain 149
Fiji 12, 42, 137
films 47, 93, 127, 153; *Golliwog* 153, 182; *Golliwog's Motor Accident 127; In*

*Gollywog Land* 97; *Jam Session* 77; *Morocco* 115; *The Old Favourite and the Ugly Golliwog* 127; *The Ragtime Golliwog Man* 127; *The Yellow Golliwog* 67; *The Yellow Teddy Bears* 67; *Tomorrow at Ten* 153, 182

firms, Allison 65; Arnott 65; Balmoral Cleanser 63-**4;** Boots 20; Cadbury 65; Carlton Ware **59**; Clarice Cliff **59**; Cooncraft 156; Crumpsall & Cardiff **59**; Dean's Rag Books Ltd 111; Glaxo Baby Milk 65; Golliwog Ices Ltd 146; Guest **65**; Hain Celestial Group 69, 82; Horlicks 53; Idris 53; Lifebuoy **96;** Lincolnshire and Norfolk Dairies 74-5; Liver Salts **180**; Lyon's Corner House 53; Merrythought 207 n332; Persil 65; Purnell & Sons 55; Quality Street 65; Rigmel 65; Rose's Lime Juice 65; Royal Doulton 58-**9**, 193 n88; Sunbeam 65; Sunlight Soap 63-**4;** Toblerone 65; Trebor **65**; Vigny 58, **92**; Vinolia Baby Soap 65; Wedgwood **49** see Roberston's

First World War 17, **18**, 19, 62, 109, 120, 135-7, 180, 198 n154; ambulance **24**; Armistice Day 158; golliwog clubs 130-**2**

Fleming, Ian 11

football 106, 133, 162

Forster, E. M. 11

France 40, 44, 94, 100, 103, 109, 113, **181**, 198 n154, 199 n175; Biarritz 135; Boulogne 143; Calais 96; Day 109; *Le Golliwogg* 59-60, **92**, 109, 114; Paris 44, 58, 109, 114, 140, 142

France, Anatole 194 n104

Francis, Clare 76

Fraser-Simpson, C. 150

Galsworthy, John 144

Gehrts, Meg 93-4

George, David Lloyd 144

Germany 12, 103, 109, 115, **142**, **150**, 151, 160, **163**; actor 93, 149; ban 159; British Army of the Rhine 109; imports 19, 60, 193 n92; music 131; Nazi Party 159

girliwog 26

Glyn, Elinor 11

Gold, Cecilia 127

gollies 10, 13, 24, 26-7, 60, 63-6, 69-82, 99-100, **101**, 102, 108, 120, 136, 157, 161, **163**, 165-8; Gollynomics **168**; history 70-2, 195 n109; market

research 73; products 73-**4**, 76, **79**; racial language 71
Golliwog Wiggle Woggle 127
golliwoggs, appropriation 51-68; artwork **2**, **22**, **24**, **36**, **124**, **141**; charms 17, 19, 119, 125-9, 130, 133, 135, 138, 151, 173, 180, 202 n235; character 84; clothing 30; clown 23; grey skin 39, 86, 171, 177; grotesqueness 26-7, 50, 173, 177; hair 27, 30, 33, 39-42, 49, 132; Lady 120; mental health 47-8, 63, 159, 177; Mr Golliwogg **2**, **22**, 37; origins 10-11, 23-52, 56, 63, 68-9, 83-6, 93, 116, 124-5, 127, 138, 140, 171-2, 175-7, 181, 183; overtaken 51; patent 51; popularity 26-7, 44-**5**, 48-9, 68, 125, 167; race 27, 30-1, 83; romance 27, 83, **84-5**, 197 n137, 159, 166; termed 40-1; The Golliwog 37; ugliness 42, 44-**5**, 46-7, 83, 91, 122, 127, 132, 173, 177; White 37, 39, **66**-7, 91, 111, 161, 197 n147, 199 n178, 204 n284; Zulu 135
Golliwogland 133
golliwogs 63; Age 145, 203 n265; Albert 199 n178; Albino 152; Boswell 153; Boutique 155; Café 155; car decorations 99, 139-40; Chalky 152; church banner 155; Club 153; colours 66-7; Days 143-4; Flag Days 144; fundraising 67, 88, 100, 120, 125, 130-5, 138, 140, 143-4, 146, 179, 180-1; garters 143; giant 155; Ginge 199 n178; Golliwog Girls **114**; Golly Girl **75**; green 55; grotesqueness 40, 46, 50, 113, 117, 132, 146, 169, hair **39**, 40, **41**, 50, 56, 67, 86-7, 90-1, 97, 102, 105, 116-117, 129, 133, 137, 146, 148, 152-3, 177, 181, 195 n107; handmade 13, 17, 19, 58, **61**-2, 66-7, 99-100, **101**, 102-3, 115, 119-120, 130, 133, 135-7, 144, 173, **179**; hat 155; hidden 10, 13-14; homes 151; Living 42, 127, 142, 149; Man 146; marionette 150; mascots 17, 44, 70, 115, 119, 127, 129, 133, 135-6, 139-40, 161-2, 166, 203 n240; Master 68; mental health 153; Miss 68; Mr Golliwog 151; Mr Smith 111; Mrs 68; music 144; politics 144-5; products 12, 58, **59**, 60, 65, **92**, **111**, **113**, **163**, **184**; race 42, 63-4, 83-108; sex 67; shops 151; skin colour 64, 67, 88-91, 105, 111; sizes 67-8; Spastic Children's Golliwog Ball 152; sports 145; stained glass **145**-6; Suzy 68; talking 130; Toy Shop 151; White 39, **66**-7, 111, 152-3, 161, 197 n147, 199 n178, 204 n284; Winston 207 n331
gollywogitis 135-6
Great Torrington 19
Greene, Evie 129
Guyan, Alexander 153

Hampshire 168; Aldershot 137; Basingstoke 156; Southsea 149
Hampson, Sylvia 13
Hertfordshire, St Albans 12
Hewson, Christina **75**
Honiton 103
Hopman, Johannes 151
Horlicks 53
Howell, Gracie 133
Hume, Marjorie 127
Hunt, Marsha 157
Huxley, Aldous 11

Iceland 110
Ilfracombe 145
immigration 14, 21, 65, 78, 108, 149, 152, 156-7, 166, 173-4
Independent Television 55, 104
India 23, 42, 88, 97, 116, 149, 198 n160; Bengal 97
Inge, William 47-8
Institute of Race Relations 156
Iraq 95; Bagdad 97
Ireland, Belfast 133, 151, **184;** Radio Golliwog 161; Ulster Defence Association 161
Isle of Wight, Cowes 193 n95
Italy 109, 205 n305

Jain, Ravi 164
Jewell, Francis 19-20
Joyce, James 11
Jumping Jim Crow 34

Kanakas 121-2
Keegan, Kevin 40
Kennedy, Jackie 11
Kent, Bruce 166
Kent, Ramsgate 19

Killerton 139
Kingskerswell, 161; Horse & Hounds 161
Kleudgen, Vera 117
Kyle, Redvers 152

Laine, Cleo 41
Langi, Jeanne 77-8
Laurel, Stan 125
Laverne, Erwin 115; Estelle 115
Law, Bonar 144
Lawson, Esther 106
Leicestershire, Leicester 157; Melton Mowbray 87
lepers, colony 12; St Giles Home for British Lepers 144
Leslie, Mark **38**
Lewis-Hind, Henriette 48
Lewis, Angelo John 48
Liberal Party 139
Lime Brothers 112-114
Lincolnshire, Lincoln 88
London 12, 26, 28, 30, 37, 39-40, 53, 58, 60, 72, 79, 90, 95, 104, 127, 130, 143, 146, 151, 152, 164; American Roller Skating Palace 127; Brixton 105; Catford 73; Chelsea 62, 67, 152; Croydon 144; Downing Street 165; Ealing 156; East End 133; Finsbury Park 106; Fortnum & Mason 156; Gravesend 132; Greater London Council 79; Greenwich London Borough Council 165; Hamleys 164; Harrods 156; Heathrow 106; Islington 132, 165; Kensington & Fulham **143**; Manor Park **132**; Marlbrough House 63; Palace Theatre **41**; Piccadilly Square 151; River Thames 95; St Giles Home for British Lepers 144; Tottenham 130; Victoria & Albert Museum 30; Victoria Palace 37; Wog Wog Boating Club 95; Young V&A 30

MacLaine, Shirley 41
Malaysia 156
Manchester 72-3, 80, 144, 150-1; Droylsden 72; exhibition 73
Mankowitz, Wolf 149
Marmalade 76

McDiarmid, John 72
McKenzie, Mike 162
Merseyside, County Council 79, 165; Liverpool 41, 118
Millar, Gertie **41**
minstrels 21, 28, **29-30**, 33-4, 37, 39, 48, 53, 63-5, 70, 77, 85-8, 100, 111-112, 129-30, 135, 143, 156, 152, 156-7, 161-2, 171-4, 177, 181; troupes 34, 87, 130
Montagu, Consuelo 135
Moore, Carrie 129
Mould, G. E. 47
music 11, 102, 112, 114, 120, 127, 129, 144, **158**; ABBA 161; Average White Band 161; Creedence Clearwater Revival 155; German **131**; 'Giggling Golliwog' 144; 'Goblin Golliwog Trees' **131**; 'Golliwog' 155, 161; 'Golliwog Cakewalk' 11; 'Golliwog on the Loose' 144; 'Gollywogs' **131**; Harmony Kings 90; 'Jumping Golliwog' 150; 'Mister Gollywog' **131**; *My Golliwog* 127; 'Rag-time golliwog man' 130; 'Ten Little Nigger Boys' 52; the Golliwogs 155; 'The Gollywog' **131**, 155

National Committee for Commonwealth Immigrants 156-7
National Committee on Racism in Children's Books 164
National Front 167
Netherlands, Peter 33
New Zealand 12, 119-20, 123, 129, 153-4, 179; Christchurch 154; Dunedin 153; Maori 123; Remuera 120
Nightingale, Charlotte 168
Nignog Club 182-3
Nixev, W. G. 142
Noades, Ron 162
Noddall, Frances 19; Kate 19
Norfolk, Gorleston-on-Sea 19
North Devon Infirmary 144
Northampton, Nottingham 54
nursiwog 26

Orton, Joe 204 n284
Orwell, George 95

Osborne, Edgar 51

Pacific Islands 121-3
Paderewski, Ignacy **49**
Pakistan 97, 116
Papua New Guinea 122-3; Samurai 122
Parlby, Cecil 140
perfume 59-60, **92**, 109, 114
Phillips, Lionel 94
plants, daffodil 12; gloxinia 12; lily 12
plays 14, 51, 125-6, 130; *Alladin* 129; *A Christmas Dream* 143; *A Visit to Nursery-Rhyme Land* 51; *Conversations with a Golliwog* 153, **154**; *Hair* 156; *Magic Apple* 51; *My Golliwog* 127; *Noddy in Toyland* 51; *Ritual for Dolls* 162; *The Golliwog* 125; *The Merry Widow* 129; *The Toys That Came Alive* 51
Plinge, Michael 202 n220
Plymouth 96-7, 140, 143, 146; Hoe 96; Spitfire Fund 146
Powell, Baden 42; Enoch 165-6
Provost, Bev 105
public pressure, 77-82; ACAFESS 165-6; Ban-The-Golliwog 77; National Committee on Racism in Children's Books 79
publications, *Adventures of Sabo* 56; *Ann's Golliwog* 149; *Detective Golly's Handbook* 74; *Ducky Daddles Party* **52**; *Dutch Doll Ditties* 56, **58**; *Father Tuck's Annual* **53-4**; *Golliwog Stories* 56; *Here Comes Noddy Again* 84; *I Love My Golly But* 165; *Jimmy Scenes from the Life of a Black Doll told by Himself* 32; *Little Black Sambo* 20, 68, 87; *Little Dolly and Her Friend Golly* **160**; *Little White Barbara* 88; *Little Yellow Wang-lo* 88; *Magic Island* 149-50; *Majollika* & Company **53**, 149; *Noddy in Toyland* 51; *Pinto's Panto* **66**, 67; *Rufty Tufty Makes a House* 150; *Rufty-Tufty the Golliwog* **54,** 149; *Shoes* **107**; *Ten Little Gollywogs* **87**; *The Adventures of Dumpy Dimple and His Dog*! 56, **57**; *The Adventures of Golly Smith* **53**, 150; *The Adventures of Two Dutch Dolls and a 'Golliwogg'* 26; *The Bad Golliwog* 149; *The Chummy Book* **56**; *The Education of Catholic Girls* 46; *The Goblin Gobblers* 56; *The Golliwog* 149; *The Golliwog News* 56; *The Golliwogg at the Sea-Side* **86**; *The Golliwogg's Airship* 26; *The Golliwog's Dreams* 56; *The Gollywog Picture Book* **54**, 149; *The Green Mummy* 122; *The Little*

*Black Doll* 54; *The Silly Golliwog and Other Stories* 51; *The So Long Book of Gollywog Tales* 149; *The Story of Little Black Mingo* 87; *The Story of Little Black Quasha* 87-8; *The Story of Little White Squibba* 88; *The Three Golliwogs* 52, 54; *The Tricky Golliwog* 52; *The White Golliwog* 161; *Toyland* 159-60; *Uncle Tom's Cabin* **43**; *Where the Dolls Lived* 56; *Wonder Book* 56

race 11, 14, 20, 27, 32-4, 42, 55, 63-65, 78, 82-108, 115, 117-120, 142, 146, 152, 159, 165, 174, 177, 182; American 86, 111, 171; blackface 21, **29**, 33-4, **35**, 125, 130, 176, 181, 201 n212; Blyton 53-5; campaign **103**; Friday 152; illustration **31**; Institute of Race Relations 156; Monday 85; perspective 99-108; Race Relations Board 55, 162; Sambo 31, 39, 54, 56, 58, 68, 85, 87-8, 105, 129, 130

Reason, Kate 13

Red Cross ambulance 30

Redsell, P. T. W. 78

Refitt, Pleasance 40

Rice, Thomas Dartmouth 34

Ritchie, Garnie 149

Robertson, James & Son 13, 26, 60, 63, 65, 67, 69-82, 102, 117, 142, 149, 157, 161, 164-6, 178, 192 n77, 195 n109; advertisements **70-2**, **77**, **79**, **81-2, 117**, **178**, 182 n77; aircraft 76; archive 69; badges 13, 73-**4**; 76, 81, 149, 161, 173; balloons 75; Black Sherlock Holmes 74; Catford 73; founder 69-70; Golden Shred Factory Girl 71; Golliberry 72; Gollicrush 72; Golliwog Productions Room 80-1; Golliwog Pudding 74; Golly Girl **75**-6; Mincemeat 74, 77, 195 n113; North American travel 70; promotional products 73-6; public pressure 77-82; *Robertson's Golly* 76; sale 69, 82; sponsorship 76; trademark 70-2, 111, 195 n109, see golly

Robinson, Phyllis 201 n209

Roosevelt, Anna 11; Eleanor 41; Franklin 11

Royal family, Alexandra 62; Camilla 63; Diana 63; Edward VII 135; Edward VIII 62; Queen Elizabeth the Queen Mother 62-3; Elizabeth II 60, 62; George V 60; George VI 60; nursery 62; Prince Henry, Duke of Gloucester 62; Prince William, Duke of Gloucester 62; Princess Royal Anne 63; Princess Margaret 42, 62; Princess Marina 63; Princess Royal Mary 62

Rushdie, Salman 105-6

Russia, Tsarevich 62

Sadler, Edna 160
Sanderson, Tessa 106
Scotland 33, 52, **56**, 63, 70, 161, 166, 176; Fancy Costume Ball 39; Glasgow 39, 161; Paisley 9, 72, 76; Peebles 166-7
Second World War 100, 102, 123, 146, 149, 164, 199 n175
sex 47, 67; birth control 47, 194 n104; syphilis 67
Shackleton, Ernest 133
Shaldon 146
Shaw, Martin 41
Sherman, Alfred 166
Shropshire, Newport 19; Shrewsbury 155
skating 127
Smith, Keith Macpherson 135
Somerset, Weston-Super-Mare 133
South Molton 144
Spreyton 37
Staffordshire 162
Stanton, Charles Butt **39**-40
Steele, Tommy 41
Steer, Sylvia 118
Stevens, Len 144
Suffolk, Sudbury 90
Surrey 135; Esher 151
Swanson, Gloria 114

Taylor, Jenny 149
teddy bears 17, 43, 55, 67-8, 72, 90-1, 99, 102-103, 149, 160, 176; Paddington 68; Rupert 68; Winnie-the-Pooh 68
Thatcher, Carole 167; Denis 165
Timperley, Frank 207 n343
Tiverton 143-4
Tommies, see Atkins
Topsy **43**
Toulouse-Lautrec, Henri de 23

United States 7, 11-12, 21, 23, 25, 28, 30, 33-4, 43-4, 48, 52, 60, 63, 65, 68, 70, 82, 86, 100, 103, 109-112, 114-116, 127, 129, 135, 143, 153, 155-6, 158, 161, 167-8, 171, 174, 181, 199 n175; Baltimore 112; California 112; Camp Golliwog 116; Chicago 116; Cincinnati 115; Cleveland 114; Connecticut 112; Detroit 114; Golliwog Club 116; Golliwog Lounges 115-116; Gollywog Tearoom 114; Hollywood 115; House of Representatives 114; Kentucky 23; Klu Klux Klan 23, 167; Minneapolis 116, 200 n189; Mississippi 129; Nebraska 125; New Orleans 116; New York 23, 33, 60, 110, 115-116; Oklahoma City 116; Omaha 112-113; Philadelphia 112, 114; Pittsburgh 114-115; San Francisco 110; Sheraton Hotels 115-116; South Carolina 188 n4; Washington 67

Upton, Bertha 26, 44, 132; Desmond 44; Florence 23-**24**, 25-52, 56, 60, 62-3, 68, 70, 83-4, 86-7 109, 112, 116, 124-5, 132, 139-40, 171, 175, 177, 190 n32, 197 n137, 201 n209

Vanbrugh, Irene 127

vessels 12; *Aurora* 133; RMS *Carinthia* 144; HMS *Crichton* **161**; *Endurance* 135; *Golliwog* 188 n4; Liverpool 118; *Queen Mary* 194 n97; *Robertson's Golly* 76

Vonnegut, Kurt 11

Wales, Brecon 13; Cardiff 58, 155; Llanfairfechan 13; Penarth 155; Penrhyn Bay 155; Prestayn 19; Treherbert 132

walliwogs 19-20

Warwickshire, Kingsbury **145**-6, 204 n267

waterwogs 14, 17-21, 34, 173, 179

Webb, Clifford 149-50

Webber, Gyll **154**

Wells, H. G. 11

West Midlands, Coventry 153, 164; Dudley 161; Walsall 155, 162; Wolverhampton 160

West Suffolk, Bury St Edmunds 54, 155-6

West Yorkshire, Leeds 135

Williams, Shirley 165

wogs 23, 78, 80, 95-7, 105, 108, 123, 155, 165, 198 notes 154, 156 & 160; Woggy 52, 97, **107**

Women's Institute 162

Woolf, Virginia 94
Wright, Haidee 47

Yaymen, Florence 130
Yealmpton 143

Zappa, Frank 41

# ALSO FROM THE MINT PRESS

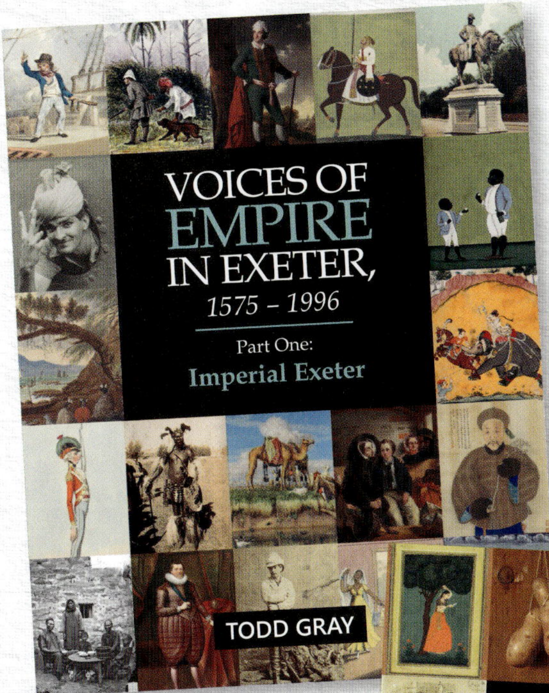


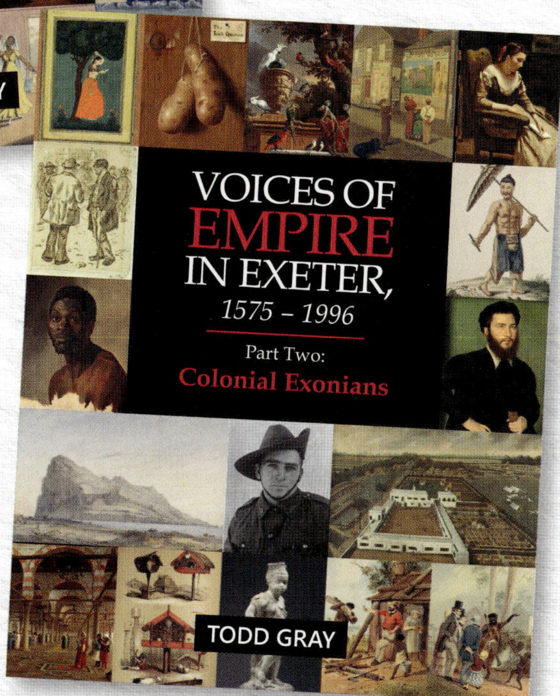

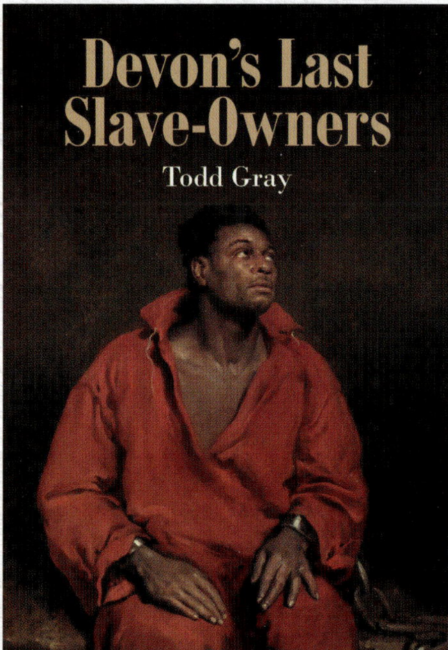
Devon's Last
Slave-Owners
Todd Gray

Todd Gray
Not One of Us
Individuals set apart by choice, circumstances,
crowds or the mob in Exeter, 1451–1952